WHAT THE WHITE RACE MAY LEARN FROM THE INDIAN

BOOKS BY GEORGE WHARTON JAMES

What the White Race May Learn from the Indian.
In and Around the Grand Canyon.
Indians of the Painted Desert Region.
In and Out of the Old Missions of California.
The Wonders of the Colorado Desert.
The Story of Scraggles.
Indian Basketry.
How to Make Indian and Other Baskets.
Travelers' Handbook to Southern California.
The Beacon Light.

GROUP OF HOPI MAIDENS AND AN OLD MAN AT MASHONGANAVI.

What the White Race May Learn from the Indian

BY

GEORGE WHARTON JAMES

AUTHOR OF "IN AND AROUND THE GRAND CANYON," "INDIAN BASKETRY," "HOW TO MAKE INDIAN AND OTHER BASKETS," "PRACTICAL BASKET MAKING," "THE INDIANS OF THE PAINTED DESERT REGION," "TRAVELERS' HAND-BOOK TO SOUTHERN CALIFORNIA," "IN AND OUT OF THE OLD MISSIONS OF CALIFORNIA," "THE STORY OF SCRAGGLES," "THE WONDERS OF THE COLORADO DESERT," "THROUGH RAMONA'S COUNTRY," "LIVING THE RADIANT LIFE," "THE BEACON LIGHT," ETC.

CHICAGO
FORBES & COMPANY
1908

The Lakeside Press
R. R. DONNELLEY & SONS COMPANY
CHICAGO

FOREWORD

I WOULD not have it thought that I commend indiscriminately everything that the Indian does and is. There are scores of things about the Indian that are reprehensible and to be avoided. Most Indians smoke, and to me the habit is a vile and nauseating one. Indians often wear filthy clothes. They are often coarse in their acts, words, and their humor. Some of their habits are repulsive. I have seen Indian boys and men maltreat helpless animals until my blood has boiled with an indignation I could not suppress, and

I have taken the animals away from them. They are generally vindictive and relentless in pursuit of their enemies. They often content themselves with impure and filthy water when a little careful labor would give them a supply of fairly good water.

Indeed, in numerous things and ways I have personally seen the Indian is not to be commended, but condemned, and his methods of life avoided. But because of this, I do not close my eyes to the many good things of his life. My reason is useless to me unless it teaches me what to accept and what to reject, and he is kin to fool who refuses to accept good from a man or a race unless in everything that man or race is perfect. There is no perfection, in man at least, on earth, and all the good I have ever received from human beings has been from imperfect men and women. So I fully recognize the imperfections of the Indian while taking lessons from him in those things that go to make life fuller, richer, better.

Neither must it be thought that everything here said of the Indians with whom I have come in contact can be said of all Indians. Indians are not all alike any more than white men and women are all alike. One can find filthy, disgusting slovens among white women, yet we do not condemn all white women on the strength of this indisputable fact. So with Indians. Some are good, some indifferent, some bad. In dealing with them as a race, a people, therefore, I do as I would with my own race, I take what to me seem to be racial characteristics, or in other words, the things that are manifested in the lives of the best men and women, and which seem to represent their habitual aims, ambitions, and desires.

This book lays no claim to completeness or thoroughness. It is merely suggestive. The field is much larger than I have gleaned over. The chapters of which the book is composed were written when away from works of reference, and merely as transcripts of the remembrances that flashed through my mind at the time of writing. Yet I believe in everything I have said I have kept strictly within the bounds of truth, and have written only that which I personally know to be fact.

The original articles from which these pages have been made were written in various desultory places, — on the cars, while traveling between the Pacific and the Atlantic, on the elevated railways of the metropolis, standing at the desk of my New York friend in his office on Broadway, even in the woods of Michigan and in the depths of the Grand Canyon. Two of the new chapters were written at the home of my friend Bass, at Bass Camp, Grand Canyon, but the main enlargement and revision has occurred at Santa Clara College, the site of the Eighth Mission in the Alta California chain of Franciscan Missions. The bells of the Mission Church have hourly rung in my ears, and the Angelus and other calls to prayer have given me sweet memories of the good old padres who founded this and the other missions, as well as shown me pictures of the devoted priests of to-day engaged in their solemn services. I have heard the merry shouts of the boys of this college at their play, for the Jesuits are the educators of the boys of the Catholic Church. Here from the precincts of this old mission, I call upon the white race to incorporate into its civilization the good things of the Indian civilization; to forsake the injurious things of its pseudo-civilized, artificial, and over-refined life, and to return to the simple, healthful, and natural life which the Indians largely lived before and after they came under the dominion of the Spanish padres.

If all or anything of that which is here presented leads any of my readers to a kinder and more honest attitude of mind towards the Indians, then I shall be thankful, and the book will have amply accomplished its mission.

George Wharton James.

Santa Clara, California, November 27, 1907.

CONTENTS

CONTENTS

CHAPTER I

THE WHITE RACE AND ITS TREATMENT OF THE INDIAN

EVER since the white race has been in power on the American continent it has regarded the Indian race — and by this I mean all the aboriginal people found here — as its inferiors in every regard. And little by little upon this hypothesis have grown up various sentiments and aphorisms which have so controlled the actions of men who never see below the surface of things, and who have no thought power of their own, that our national literature has become impregnated with the fiendish conception that "the only good Indian is the dead Indian." The exploits of a certain class of scouts and Indian-hunters have been lauded in books without number, so that even schoolboys are found each year running away west, each with a belt of cartridges around his waist and a revolver in his hip pocket, for the purpose of *hunting Indians*. Good men and women, people of the highest character, are found to be possessed of an antipathy towards the Indian that is neither moral nor christian. Men of the highest integrity in ordinary affairs will argue forcefully and with an apparent confidence in the justice of their plea that the Indian has no rights in this country that we are bound to respect. They are here merely on sufferance, and whatever the United States government does for them is pure and disinterested philanthropy, for which the Indian should be only grateful and humble.

To me this is a damnable state of affairs. If prior possession entitles one to any right in land, then the Indian owns the land of the United States by prior right. The so-called argument that because the Indian is not wisely *using* the land, and that therefore he stands in the way of progress and must be removed, and further, that we, the people of the United States, are the providentially appointed instruments for that removal, is to me so sophistical, so manifestly insincere, so horribly cruel, that I have little patience either to listen or reply to it.

If this be true, what about the vast holders of land whom our laws cherish and protect? Are they holding the land for useful and good purposes? Are they "helping on the cause of civilization" by their merciless and grasping control of the millions of acres they have generally so unlawfully and immorally secured? Thousands, nay millions, of acres are held by comparatively few men, without one thought for the common good. The only idea in the minds of these men is the selfish one: "What can I make out of it?"

Let us be honest with ourselves and call things by their proper names in our treatment of the weaker race. If the Indian is in the way and we are determined to take his land from him, let us at least be manly enough to recognize ourselves as thieves and robbers, and do the act as the old barons of Europe used to do it, by force of arms, fairly and cheerfully: "You have these broad acres: I want them. I challenge you to hold them: to the victor belongs the spoils." Then the joist began. And he who was the stronger gained the acres and the castle.

Let us go to the Indian and say: "I want your lands, your hunting-grounds, your forests, your waterholes, your springs, your rivers, your corn-fields, your mountains, your canyons. I need them for my own use. I am stronger than you; there are more of us than there are of you. I've got to have them. You will have to do with less. I'm going to take them;" and then proceed to the robbery. But let us be above the contemptible meanness of calling our theft "benevolent assimilation," or "manifest destiny," or "seeking the higher good of the Indian." A nation as well as a race may do scoundrel acts, but let it not add to its other evil the contemptible crime of conscious hypocrisy. The unconscious hypocrite is to be pitied as well as shaken out of his hypocrisy, but the conscious hypocrite is a stench in the nostrils of all honest men and women. The major part of the common people of the United States have been unconscious of the hypocritical treatment that has been accorded the Indians by their leaders, whether these leaders were elected or appointed officials or self-elected philanthropists and reformers. Hence, while I would "shake them up" and make them conscious of their share in the nation's hypocrisy, I have no feeling of condemnation for them. On the other hand, I feel towards the conscious humbugs and hypocrites, who use the Indian as a cloak for their own selfish aggrandizement and advancement, as the Lord is said to have felt toward the lukewarm churches when He exclaimed: "I will spew thee out of my mouth."

In our treatment of the Indian we have been liars, thieves, corrupters of the morals of their women, debauchers of their maidens, degraders of their young manhood, perjurers, and murderers. We have lied to them about our good, pacific, and honorable intentions; we have made promises to them that we never intended to keep — made them simply to gain our own selfish and mercenary ends in the easiest possible way, and then have repudiated our promises without conscience and without remorse. We have stolen from them nearly all they had of lands and worldly possessions. Only two or three years ago I was present when a Havasupai Indian was arrested for having shot a deer out of season, taken before the courts and heavily fined, when his own father had roamed over the region hunting, as his ancestors had done for centuries before, ere there were any white men's laws or courts forbidding them to do what was as natural for them to do as it was to drink of the water they found, eat of the fruits and berries they passed, or breathe the air as they rode along. The law of the white man in reference to deer and antelope hunting is based upon the selfishness of the white man, who in a few generations has slain every buffalo, most of the mountain sheep, elk, moose, and left but a comparative remnant of deer and antelope. The Indian has never needed such laws. He has always been unselfish enough to leave a sufficient number of this wild game for breeding purposes, or, if it was not unselfishness that commanded his restraint, his own self-interest in piling up meat was sacrificed to the general good of his people who required meat also, and must be able to secure it each year. Hence, to-day we shut off by law the normal and natural source of meat supply of the Indian, without any consultation with him, and absolutely without recourse or redress, because we ourselves — the white race — are so unmitigatedly selfish, so mercenary, so indifferent to the future needs of the race, that without such law we would kill off all the wild game in a few short years.

Then who is there who has studied the Indian and the white man's relation to him, who does not know of the vile treatment the married women and maidens

A WALLAPAI BASKET WEAVER.

alike have received at the hands of the "superior" people. Let the story of the devilish debaucheries of young Indian girls by Indian agents and teachers be fully written, and even the most violent defamers of Indians would be compelled to hang their heads with shame. To those who know, the name of Perris —

a southern California Indian school — brings up memories of this class of crime that make one's blood hot against the white fiend who perpetrated them, and I am now as I write near to the Havasupai reservation in northern Arizona, where one of the teachers had to leave surreptitiously because of his discovered immoralities with Indian women and girls. Only a decade ago the name of the Wallapai woman was almost synonymous with immorality because of the degrading influences of white men, and one of the most pathetic things I ever heard was the hopeless "What can we do about it?" of an Indian chief on the Colorado desert, when I spoke to him of the demoralization of the women of his people. In effect his reply was: "The whites have so driven us to the wall that we are often hungry, and it is far easier to be immoral than to go hungry."

Then, read the reports of the various Indian agents throughout the country who have sought to enforce the laws against whites selling liquor to Indians. Officials and courts alike have often been supine and indifferent to the Indian's welfare, and have generally shown far more desire to protect the white man in his "vested interests" than to protect the young men of the Indian tribes against the evil influences of liquor. Again and again I have been in Indian councils and heard the old men declaim against the white man's fire-water. The Havasupais declare it to be *han-a-to-op-o-gi*, "very bad," the Navahos *da-shon-de*, "of the Evil One," while one and all insist that their young men shall be kept from its demoralizing influence. Yet there is seldom a *fiesta* at which some vile white wretch is not willing to sell his own soul, and violate the laws of whites and Indians alike,

A SKILLED HOPI BASKET WEAVER.

in order to gain a little dirty pelf by providing some abominable decoction which he sells as whisky to those whose moral stamina is not strong enough to withstand the temptation.

And as for perjury in our dealings with Indians: read the records of broken treaties, violated pledges, and disregarded vows noted by Helen Hunt Jackson in her "Century of Dishonor," and then say whether the charge is not sustained.

Yet, when the Indian has dared to resent the cruel and abominable treatment accorded to him in so many instances and in such fearful variety, he has been called "treacherous, vindictive, fiendish, murderous," because, in his just and righteous indignation and wrath, he has risen and determined to slay all he could find of the hated white race. No doubt his warfare has not always been civilized. Why should it be? How could it be? He is not civilized. He knows nothing of "christian" principles in a war which "christian" people have forced upon him as an act of self-defense. He is a savage, battling with savage ferocity, savage determination, to keep his home, that of his ancestors, for himself, his children, and their children. Oom Paul Kruger told the British that if they forced a war upon the Boers for the possession of the Transvaal, they would win it at a price that would "stagger humanity." Yet thousands of good Americans honored Oom Paul for his "bravery," his "patriotism," his "god-like determination to stand for the rights of his people." But if our Indian does the same thing in the defense of his home and slaughters a lot of soldiers sent to drive him away, he is guilty of murderous treachery; his killings are "massacres," and he must be exterminated as speedily as possible.

Who ever hears any other than the term "massacre" applied to the death of Custer and his soldiers? The "Custer massacre" is as "familiar as household words." Yet what is a massacre? Webster says: "1. The killing of a considerable number of human beings under circumstances of atrocity or cruelty, or contrary to the usages of civilized people. 2. Murder." With such definitions in view, look at the facts of the case. I would not have it understood in what I say that I am condemning Custer. He was a general under orders, and as a dutiful servant he was endeavoring to carry them out. (The debatable question as to whether he was obeying or disregarding orders I leave for military men themselves to settle.) It is not Custer, or any other one individual, that I am condemning, but the public, national policy. Custer's army was ordered to proceed against these men, and forcibly remove them from the place they had chosen as their home — and which had been theirs for centuries before a white man ever trod this continent — and take them to a reservation which they disliked, and in the choice of which their wishes, desires, or comfort had in no way been consulted. The white soldiers were armed, and it is well known that they intended to use these arms. Could they have come upon the Indians by stealth, or by some stratagem, they would have done so without any compunctions of conscience, and no one would ever have thought of administering a rebuke to them, even though in the fight that would undoubtedly have ensued every Indian had been slain. It would have been heralded as a glorious victory, and we should have thanked God for His goodness in directing our soldiers in their "honorable" warfare. But unfortunately, the incident turned in another direction.

The would-be captors were the caught; the would-be surprisers were the surprised; the would-be slayers were the slain. Custer and his band of men, brave and gallant as United States soldiers generally are, — and I would resent with heat any slanderous remark to the contrary, — were surrounded, surprised, and slain to a man.

Weep at the grave of Custer; weep at the graves of his men; weep with the widows and orphans of those suddenly surprised and slain soldiers. My own tears have fallen many a time as I have read and reread the details of that awful tragedy; but still, in the weeping do not be dishonest and ungenerous to the victors, — Indians though they were. Upon the testimony of no less an authority than General Charles King, who has known the Sioux personally and intimately for years, they were ever the hospitable friends of the white race, until a post commander, — whose name should be pilloried for the execration of the nation,— imbued with the idea that the only good Indian was the dead Indian, betrayed and slew in cold blood a number of them who had trusted to his promises and placed themselves in his hands. The result was, that the whole tribe took this slaughter to their own hearts, as any true patriots would have done, and from that day to this the major part of the Sioux have hated the white race with the undying, bitter hatred of the vindictive savage.

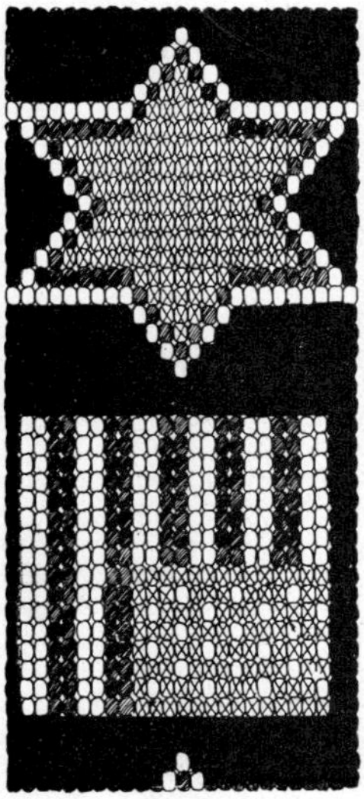

INDIAN BEADWORK OF INTERESTING DESIGN.

Again and again when I have visited Indian schools the thoughtful youths and maidens have come to me with complaints about the American history they were compelled to study. In their simple, almost colorless way of expressing themselves, a bystander would never dream of the fierce anger that was raging within, but which I was too experienced in Indian character not to perceive. Listen to what some of them have said: "When we read in the United States history of white men fighting to defend their families, their homes, their corn-fields, their towns, and their hunting-grounds, they are always called 'patriots,' and the children are urged to follow the example of these brave, noble, and gallant men. But when Indians — our ancestors, even our own parents — have fought to defend us and our homes, corn-fields, and hunting-grounds they are called vindictive and merciless savages, bloody murderers, and everything else that is vile. You are the Indians' friend: will you not some time please write for us a United States history that will not teach us such wicked and cruel falsehoods about our forefathers because they loved their homes enough to fight for them — even against such powerful foes as you have been." And I have vowed that if ever I have time and strength and feel competent to do it, I will write such a history.

Yet this is by no means all the charge I have to make against my own race in its treatment of the Indian. Not content with depriving him of his worldly possessions, we have added insult to injury, and administered a far deeper and more cutting wound to him by denying to him and his wives and daughters the moral, poetical, and spiritual qualities they possess. To many of the superior (!) race this is utter nonsense. The idea that an Indian has any feelings to be hurt! How ridiculous! Yet I make the assertion, fearless of successful contradiction, that many Indians feel more keenly this ignoring of the good, the poetic, the æsthetic, the religious or spiritual qualities they possess than they do the physical wrongs that have been inflicted upon them. As a race, we are prejudiced, bigoted, and "big-headed" when looking upon any other race. We come by our prejudices naturally. The Englishman looks down upon the "frog-eating Frenchman," and used to say he could lick ten or a dozen such. The Frenchman and Englishman both scoff at the beer-drinking German and the stolid Dutchman, yet France has to remember Sedan, and England still smarts at the name of Van Tromp. The fact is that no nation can afford to look down upon another, any more than any civilization can afford to crow over another. Each has its own virtues, its own "goods," its own advantages. France, England, Germany, America, have never equaled, much less surpassed, the architecture of Greece, Egypt, and Rome. The United States, with all its brag and boast, has never had a poet equal to old blind Homer or the Italian Dante. Germany's Goethe is worthy to stand side by side with England's Shakspere, and the architecture of the rude and vulgar "Goths" is the supremest crown of all building in the proud and conceited English-speaking "Mother Country."

INDIAN BEADWORK.

And so have I learned to look at the Indian. He

has many things that we can take to our advantage and profit, and some of these have been presented in the following pages. In the next chapter I have a few necessary reservations and observations to make which I trust the patience of the reader will permit him carefully to consider.

CHAPTER II

THE WHITE RACE AND ITS CIVILIZATION

I AM by no means a blind worshiper of our so-called "higher" and "advanced" civilization. I do not think we have advanced yet as far as the Greeks in some things. Our civilization, in many respects, is sham, shoddy, gingerbread, tinsel, false, showy, meretricious, deceptive. If I were making this book an arraignment of our civilization there would be no lack of counts in the indictment, and a plethora of evidence could be found to justify each charge.

INDIAN BEADWORK OF RATTLESNAKE DESIGN.

As a nation, we do not know how to eat rationally; few people sleep as they should; our drinking habits could not be much worse; our clothing is stiff, formal, conventional, hideous, and unhealthful; our headgear the delirium tremens of silliness. Much of our architecture is weakly imitative, flimsy, without dignity, character, or stability; much of our religion a profession rather than a life; our scholastic system turns out anæmic and half-trained pupils who are forceful demonstrators of the truth that "a little knowledge is a dangerous thing." And as for our legal system, if a body of lunatics from the nearest asylum could not concoct for us a better hash of jurisprudence than now curses our citizenship I should be surprised. No honest person, whether of the law or out of it, denies that "law"—which Browning so forcefully satirizes as "the patent truth-extracting process,"—has become a system of formalism, of precedent, of convention, of technicality. A case may be tried, and cost the city, county, or state thousands of dollars; a decision rendered, and yet, *upon a mere technicality that does not affect the real merits of the case one iota*, the decision will be reversed, and either the culprit—whose guilt no one denies—is discharged, or a new trial, with its attendant expense, is ordered. The folly of such a system! The sheer idiocy of *men* wasting time and strength and energy upon such puerile foolishness. I verily believe the world would be bettered if the whole legal system, from supreme court of the United States down to pettiest justice court, could be abolished at one blow, and a reversion made to the decisions of the old men of each community known for their good common sense, fearlessness, and integrity.

It may be possible that some who read these words will deem me an incontinent and general railer against our civilization. Such a conclusion would be an egregious error. I rail against nothing in it but that which I deem bad,—bad in its effect upon the bodies, minds, or souls of its citizens. I do not rail against the wireless telegraph, the ocean cables, the railway, the telephone, the phonograph, the pianoforte, the automobile, the ice machine, refrigerating machine, gas light, gas for heating and cooking, the electric light and heater, electric railways, newspapers, magazines, books, and the thousand and one things for which this age and civilization of ours is noted. But I do rail against the abuse and perversion of these things. I do rail against the system that permits gamblers to swindle the common people by watering the stock of wireless telegraphy, cable, railway, or other companies. I enjoy some phonographs amazingly, but I rail against my neighbor's running his phonograph all night. I think coal-oil a good thing, but I rail against the civilization that allows a few men to so control this God-given natural product that they can amass in a few short years for-

RAMONA AND HER STAR BASKET.

tunes that so far transcend the fortunes of the kings of ancient times that they make the wealth of Crœsus look like "thirty cents." I believe thoroughly in education; but I rail earnestly, sincerely, and constantly against that so-called education (with which nearly all our present systems are more or less allied) of valuing the embalmed knowledge of books more than the personal, practical, experimental knowledge of the things themselves. I enjoy books, and would have a library as large as that of the British Museum if I could afford it; but I rail persistently against the civilization that leads its members to accept things they find in books more than the things they think out for themselves. Joaquin Miller seemed to say a rude and foolish thing when he answered Elbert Hubbard's question, "Where are your books?" with a curt, "To hell with books. When I want a book I write one;" and yet he really expressed a deep and profound thought. He wanted to show his absolute contempt for the idea that we read books in order to help thought. The fact is, the reading too much in books, and of too many books, is a definite hindrance to thought — a positive preventive of thought. I do not believe in predigested food for either body, mind, or soul; hence I am opposed to those features of our civilization that give us food that needs only to be swallowed (not masticated and enjoyed) to supply nutriment; that give us thought all ready prepared for us that we must accept or be regarded as uneducated; those crumbs of social customs that a frivolous four hundred condescend to allow to fall from their tables to us, and that we must observe or be ostracized as "boors" and "vulgar"; and those features of our theological system that give us predigested spiritual food that we must accept and follow or be damned. I am willing to go and feed with the Scotch and the horses (*vide* Johnson's foolish remark about oatmeal), and be regarded as uneducated and be ostracized both as a boor and a vulgarian, and even be damned in words, which, thank God, is quite as far as He allows any one human being to "damn" another. For I am opposed to these things one and all.

I am not a pessimist about our civilization: I am an optimist. Yet I often find my optimism strongly tinged with pessimistic color. And how can it be otherwise?

Can any thinking man have much respect — any, in fact — for that phase of his civilization which permits the building of colossal fortunes by the monopolization of the sale of *necessities*, when the poor who are compelled to buy these necessities are growing poorer and poorer each year?

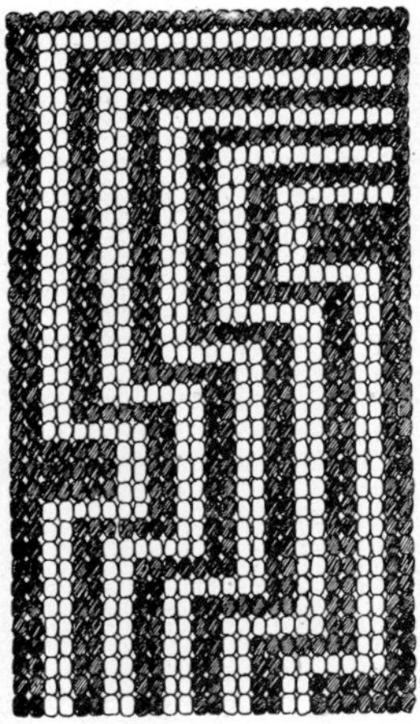

INDIAN BEADWORK OF GREEK FRET DESIGN.

Can I respect any civilization that for the 125 years of its existence has refused to pass laws for the preservation of the purity of the food of its poor? The rich can buy what and where they choose, but for the whole period of our existence we have been so bound, hand and foot, by the money-makers who have vitiated our food supply that they might add a few more millions to their dirty hoard of ungodly dollars that we have closed our eyes to the physical and spiritual demoralization that has come to the poor by the poisoned concoctions handed out to them — under protection of United States laws — as foods.

Can I respect an educational institution that educates the minds of its children at the expense of their bodies? That has so little common sense and good judgment as to be putting its children through fierce competitive examinations when they should be strengthening their bodies at the critical age of adolescence?

Can I bow down before the civilization whose

highest educational establishments — Harvard, Yale, Princeton, Cornell, New York, Columbia, Johns Hopkins, followed by hosts of others of lesser institutions — every year send out from five to thirty per cent of their students broken down in health? What is the good of all the book-learning that all the ages have amassed unless one has physical health to enjoy it? Only this last year a Harvard graduate came to me who had taken high degree in the study of law and was adjudged eminently prepared to begin to practice his profession. But his health was gone. He was a nervous and physical wreck. His physicians commanded complete rest for a year, and suggested that five years would be none too long for him to spend in recuperation. When this young man asked me to give him my candid expressions upon the matter, I asked him if he thought imbeciles could have made a worse mess of his "education" than had the present system, which had cultivated his intellect, but so disregarded the needs of his body that his intellect was powerless to act.

Let the wails of agony of the uncounted dead who have been hurried to their graves by this idolatrous worship of a senseless, godless, heartless Moloch called "education" answer for me when people ask me to respect this feature of our higher civilization, and to these wails let there be added those of awakened parents who have seen, when too late, into what acts akin to murder their blind worship of this idol had led them. Add to these the cries of pain from ten thousand beds of affliction occupied by those still living, but whose bodies have "broken down" as the result of "over-study."

Then add to the vast pyramid of woe the heartaches of hopes banished, of ambitions thwarted, of desires and aims completely lost, and one can well understand why I am not a worshiper at this shrine. If I were to choose — as every parent must for his young children who are not yet capable of thought — between a happy, because physically healthy, life,

A SABOBA INDIAN WITH BASKET IN WHICH IS SYMBOLIZED THE HISTORY OF HIS TRIBE.

though uneducated by the schools, and an educated and unhappy, because unhealthy, life for children, I would say: Give me ignorance (of books and schools) and health, rather than education (of books and schools) and a broken down, nervous, irritable body. But it is by no means necessary to have uneducated children, even though they should never see a school. While I now write (I am enjoying a few days on the "rim" of the Grand Canyon) I am meeting daily a remarkable family. The man is far above the average in *scholastic* and book *education.* He is a distinguished physician, known not only within the bounds of his own large state, but throughout the whole United States and Europe; his methods are largely approved by men at the head of the profession, and his lucrative and enormous practice demonstrates the success of his system, with the complete approval of the most conservative of his rigidly conservative profession. He was until quite recently a professor in one of the largest universities of the United States, and was therefore competent from inside knowledge to pass judgment upon the methods of the highest educational establishments. He has money enough to place his two daughters wherever he chooses, and to spend most of his time near them. Yet he has deliberately (and I think most wisely) kept them out of school, and made the strength and vigor of their bodies his first consideration. Both ride horseback (astride, of course) with the poise and confidence of skilled vaqueros; both can undertake long journeys, horseback or afoot, that would exhaust most young men students; and now at 15 and 17 years of age they are models of physical health and beauty, and at the same time the elder sister is *better* educated in the practical, sane, useful, living affairs of men and women than any girl of her age I have ever met. I take this object-lesson, therefore, as another demonstration of the truth of my position, and again I refuse to bow down before the great fetich of our modern civilization — "scholastic education."

There have been wonderful civilizations in the past, — Persia, Asia Minor, Etruria, Greece, Rome, Egypt, the Moors, — and yet they are gone. A few remnants are left to us in desert temples, sand-buried proplyæ, dug-up vases and carvings, glorious architecture, sublime marbles, and soul-stirring literature. Where are the peoples who created these things? Why could they not propagate their kind sufficiently well to at least keep their races intact, and hold what they had gained? We know they did not do it. Why? Call it moral or physical deterioration, or both, it is an undeniable fact that physical weakness rendered the descendants of these peoples incapable of living upon their ancestors' high planes, or made them an easy prey to a stronger and more vigorous race. I am fully inclined to the belief that it was their moral declensions that led to their physical deterioration; yet I also firmly believe that a better and truer morality can be sustained upon a healthy and vigorous body than upon one which is diseased and enervated.

Hence I plead, with intense earnestness, for a better physical life for our growing boys and girls, our young men and women, and especially for our prospective parents. Healthy progeny cannot be expected from diseased stock. The fathers and mothers of the race must be strengthened physically. Every child should be healthily, happily, and cheerfully *born*, as well as *borne*. The sunshine of love should smile down from the faces of both parents into the child's eyes the first moment of its life. Thus the elixir of joy enters its heart, and joy is as essential to the proper development of a child as sunshine is to that of a flower. This

DAT-SO-LA-LE, THE WASHOE BASKET WEAVER, SOME OF WHOSE BASKETS HAVE SOLD FOR FABULOUS PRICES.

is a physical world, even though it be only passing phenomena, and upon its recognition much of our happiness depends. Our Christian Science friends see in physical inharmony only an error of mortal mind, to be demonstrated over by divine mind. That demonstration, however, produces the effect we call physical health. This is what I long for, seek after, strive for, both for myself, my family, my children, my race. Any and all means that can successfully be used to promote that end I believe in and heartily commend. Let us call it what we will, and attain it as how we may, the desirable thing in our national and individual life to-day is health, — health of the whole man, body, mind, soul. Because I firmly believe the Indians have ideas that, if carried out, will aid us to attain this glorious object, I have dared to suggest that this proud and haughty white race may sit at their feet and learn of them.

I myself began life handicapped with serious ill health, and for twenty-two years was seldom free from pain. Nervous irritability required constant battling. But when I began to realize the benefit of life spent in God's great out-of-doors, and devoted much of my time to climbing up and down steep canyon walls, riding over the plains and mountains of Nevada and California, wandering through the aseptic wastes of the deserts of the Southwest, rowing and swimming in the waters of the great Colorado River, sleeping nightly in the open air, and in addition, coming in intimate contact with many tribes of Indians, and learning from them how to live a simple, natural, and therefore healthy life, — these things not only gave to me almost perfect health, but have suggested the material of which this book is made.

CHAPTER III

THE INDIAN AND NASAL AND DEEP BREATHING

THE Indian believes absolutely in nasal breathing. Again and again I have seen the Indian mother, as soon as her child was born, watch it to see if it breathed properly. If not, she would at once pinch the child's lips together and keep them pinched until the breath was taken in and exhaled easily and naturally through the nostrils. If this did not answer, I have watched her as she took a strip of buckskin and tied it as a bandage below the chin and over the crown of the head, forcing the jaws together, and then with another bandage of buckskin she covered the lips of the little one. Thus the habit of nasal breathing was formed immediately the child saw the light, and it knew no other method.

As one walks through the streets of every large city, he sees the dull and vacant eye, the inert face, of the mouth-breather; for, as every physician well knows, the mouth-breather suffers from lack of memory and a general dullness of the intellect. Not only that, but he habitually submits himself to unnecessary risks of disease. In breathing through the nose, the disease germs, which abound in our city streets and are sent floating through the air by every passing wind, are caught by the gluey mucus or the capillaries of the mucous membranes. The wavy air passages of the nose lead one to assume that they are so constructed expressly for this purpose, as the germs, if they escape being caught at one angle, are pretty sure to be trapped in turning another. When this mucus is expelled in the act of "blowing the nose," the germs go with it, and disease is prevented. But when these germs are taken in through the mouth, they go directly into the throat, the bronchial tubes, and the lungs, and if they are lively and strong, they lodge there and take

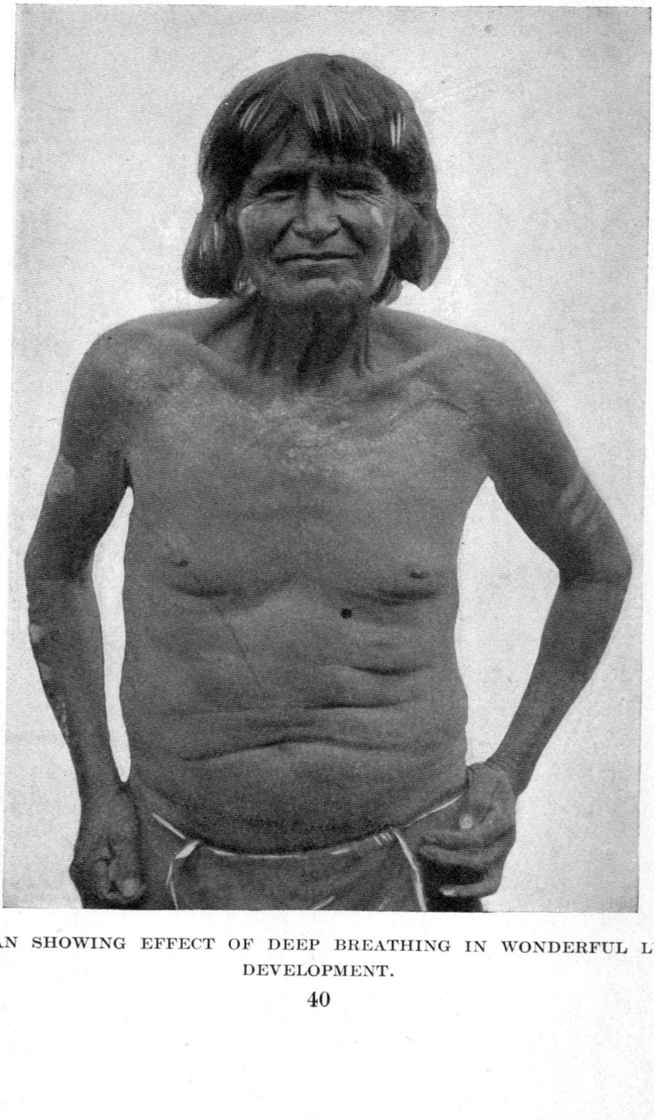

INDIAN SHOWING EFFECT OF DEEP BREATHING IN WONDERFUL LUNG DEVELOPMENT.

root and propagate with such fearful rapidity that in a very short time a new patient with tuberculosis, diphtheria, typhoid, or some other disease, is created. Hence, emulate the Indian. Breathe through your nose; do not use it as an organ of speech. At the same time that you care for yourself, watch your children, and even if you have to bandage them up while they are asleep, as the Indians do, compel them to form early this useful and healthful habit of nasal breathing.

But not only do the Indians breathe through the nose: they are also experts in the art of deep breathing. The exercises that are given in open-air deep breathing at the Battle Creek sanitarium each morning show that we are learning this useful and beneficial habit from them. When I first began to visit the Hopis, in northern Arizona, I was awakened every morning in the wee sma' hours, as I slept in my blankets in the open at the foot of the mesa upon which the towns are located, by cow-bells, as if a number of cows were being driven out to pasture. But in the daytime I could see no cows nor any evidence of their existence. When I asked where they were, my questions brought forth nothing but a wondering stare. Cows? They had no cows. What did I mean? Then I explained about the bells, and as I explained, a merry laugh burst upon my ears. "Cows? Those are not cows. To-morrow morning when you hear them, you jump up and watch." I did so, and to my amazement I saw fleeing through the early morning dusk a score (more or less) of naked youths, on each one of whom a cow-bell was dangling from a rope or strap around his waist. Later I learned this running was done as a matter of religion. Every young man was required to run ten, fifteen, twenty miles, and even double this distance, upon certain allotted mornings, as a matter of religion. This develops a lung capacity that is nothing short of marvelous.

This great lung capacity is in itself a great source of health, vim, energy, and power. It means the power to take in a larger supply of oxygen to purify and vivify the blood. Half the people of our cities do not know what real true life is, because their blood is not well enough oxygenated. The people who are full of life and exuberance and power — the men and women who accomplish things — generally have large lung capacity, or else have the faculty of using all they have to the best advantage.

To a public speaker, a singer, a lawyer, a preacher, or a teacher, this large lung capacity is invaluable; for, all things else being equal, the voice itself will possess a clearer, more resonant quality if the lungs, the abdomen, and the diaphragm are full of, or stretched out by, plenty of air. These act as a resonant sounding-chamber which increases the carrying quality of the voice to a wonderful extent.

For years I have watched with keenest observation all our greatest operatic singers, actors, orators, and public speakers, and those who possess the sweet and resonant voices are the ones who breathe deep and own and control these capacious lungs. Only a few weeks ago I went to hear Sarah Bernhardt, the world's most wonderful actress, who at sixty-three years of age still entrances thousands, not only by the wonder of her art, but by the marvelous quality of her voice. What did I find? A woman who has learned this lesson of deep breathing as the Indians breathe. She breathes well down, filling the lungs so that they thrust out the ribs. She has no waist-line, her body descending (as does that of the Venus) in an almost straight line from armpit to hips. The result is, that, with such a resonant air cavity, she scarcely raises her voice above the conversational pitch, and yet it is easily heard by two or three thousand people.

It is needless to add that every Indian woman is intelligent enough to value health, lung capacity, and the power to speak with force, vigor, and energy more than she values "fashionable appearance"; hence none of them can be found in their native condition foolish enough to wear corsets.

I never knew an Indian woman who "needed a corset, don't you know, to brace her up, to sustain her weak back." Of course, if a white woman is large and fleshy, and values appearance more than health, I suppose she will have her own way anyhow, but this other reason that women give for the use of the corset I never heard fall from the lips of an Indian woman. She is strong and well, and needs no artificial support. I regret very much to see that while sensible women are giving up the corset, or at least materially loosening its strings, men are beginning to wear belts in place of suspenders. It is just as injurious to a man to encircle his waist and squeeze together the vital organs as it is to a woman. It is bad, absolutely, completely, thoroughly bad, at all times, in all circumstances, for all people. The wasp-like waist, whether in men or women, is a sign either of recklessness, gross ignorance, or deliberate preference for a false figure over a normal one and health. The hips are a most important part of a human being's anatomy. As Dr. Kellogg has well said:

"No physical endowment is of more importance for a long and a vigorous life than capacious lungs.

The intensity and efficiency of an individual's life depend very largely upon the amount of air he habitually passes in and out of his lungs, just as the intensity of a fire, granting plenty of fuel, depends upon the rate at which the air is brought in contact with the fuel. It has been found that lung capacity depends very largely upon the height; thus, the taller a person the greater his lung capacity, other things being equal. The following table shows the lung capacity, or rather the amount of air which can be forced out of the lungs, the so-called vital capacity, for men of different heights:

Height Inches	Weight Pounds	Vital Capacity Cubic Inches
64	115	205
65	126	228
66	126	230
67	133	244
68	134	248
69	140	254
70	141	256
71	150	272
72	151	287

"The proper time for the development of the chest is in childhood and in youth. The best of all means for increasing the chest capacity is running and active sports of all sorts. Mountain climbing, going up and down stairs, and all kinds of exercises which produce strong breathing movements are effective means of chest development. Exercises of this nature are far superior to breathing exercises, so-called, of whatever sort. Breathing exercises in which the lungs are forcibly compelled to take in more than the ordinary amount of air very soon become tiresome. The effort is wholly voluntary, and the muscles soon weary. When, however, a thirst for air is created by some active exercise which fills the blood with carbonic-acid gas, so that deeper and more rapid breathing is necessary to rid the body of this poisonous gas and to take in a supply of oxygen in its place, the act of breathing is no longer difficult, embarrassing, or tiresome, but is, on the other hand, a pleasure and a gratification. The impulse which comes from within, from the so-called respiratory centers, so excites the respiratory muscles that they cause the chest to execute the strongest breathing movements with the greatest ease, ventilating every portion of the lungs, filling every air-cell to its utmost capacity.

ONE OF THE TRAILS UP WHICH THE HOPIS CLIMB AT FULL SPEED.

"Runners always have large and active chests, whereas sedentary persons have chests of limited capacity and rigid walls. When a chest is not stretched to its utmost capacity many times daily, it rapidly loses its flexibility. This is especially true after the age of thirty. In persons who have passed middle life, the rigidity of the chest is so great that there can be no very considerable increase in size. By development of the respiratory muscles the chest capacity may be to some degree increased, but the proper time for chest development is in childhood and youth. At this period, also, the integrity of the heart renders possible without injury those vigorous exercises which are essential to secure the highest degree of chest development.

"Probably the best of all exercises for the development of the chest and breathing powers is swimming. The position of the body, the head held well back and the chest well forward, and the active movements of the arms and limbs render swimming a most efficient breathing exercise. The contact of cold water with the skin also actively stimulates the movement of the chest, while at the same time it renders possible prolonged and vigorous muscular movements by increasing the energy and activity of the muscles.

"Special breathing exercises, as well as those active muscular movements which induce a thirst for air, are beneficial to the lungs by maintaining the flexibility of the chest, strengthening the respiratory muscles, and ventilating the lungs. These movements also exercise a most extraordinary beneficial effect upon the stomach, liver, and other organs which lie below the diaphragm. Each time the diaphragm contracts, it gives the liver, stomach, and adjacent organs a hearty squeeze, so to speak, emptying out the blood contained in these parts as one may by compression empty a moist sponge. All movements which increase the strength of the abdominal muscles are an important means of aiding and improving the breathing function."

From this it will be seen, therefore, that everything that prevents the full and free exercise of the lungs, especially in the lower portions, is of direct injury to the body. Men need all the lung capacity and power they can gain in order to sustain their energy in the battle of life; and women, especially young women, who are to become the future mothers of the race, should be taught that the art of healthy, deep breathing is one of the fine arts, and the most important one that they can learn.

NAVAHO BLANKET WEAVER IN HER OPEN AIR WORK-SHOP.

CHAPTER IV

THE INDIAN AND OUT-OF-DOOR LIFE

THE Indian is an absolute believer in the virtue of the outdoor life, not as an occasional thing, but as his regular, set, uniform habit. He *lives* out of doors; not only does his body remain in the open, but his mind, his soul, are ever also there. Except in the very cold weather his house is free to every breeze that blows. He laughs at "drafts." "Catching cold" is a something of which he knows absolutely nothing. When he learns of white people shutting themselves up in houses into which the fresh, pure, free air of the plains and deserts, often laden with the healthful odors of the pines, firs, balsams of the forest, cannot come, he shakes his head at the folly, and feels as one would if he saw a man slamming his door in the face of his best friend. Virtually he sleeps out of doors, eats out of doors, works out of doors. When the women make their baskets and pottery, it is always out of doors, and their best beadwork is always done in the open. The men make their bows and arrows, dress their buckskin, make their moccasins and buckskin clothes, and perform nearly all their ceremonials out of doors.

Our greatest scientific fighters against tuberculosis are emulating the Indian in the fact that even in the winter of the East they advocate that their patients sleep out of doors. Pure air, and abundance of it, is their cry.

"Taking cold" comes, not from breathing "night air," but generally from inflammation of the mucous membranes caused by impure air,— the air of a heated room from which all the pure air has been exhausted by being breathed again and again into the lungs of its deluded occupants, each exhalation sending with it a fresh amount of poison to vitiate the little good that remains.

Men often go to gymnasiums in the city to get exercise. The air is vitiated by the presence of others, and as respiration is increased by the exercise, impure air is taken into the lungs, and the prime object of the exercise is defeated. For it is not so much to develop muscles as it is to stimulate the general action of the whole body that gymnastics should be indulged in. Vigorous exercise demands deep breathing; if the air breathed is pure, the blood thereby becomes more oxygenated or vivified. As this vitalized blood circulates, it carries its life-giving new strength and energy to every part of the body, so that the whole man feels the increased vigor. But let the air be impure, death instead of life is given to the blood. Hence, where possible, all vigorous exercise should be taken out of doors in the pure air and sunlight, and if this is not possible, every door, window, and avenue through which outside air can be brought inside should be placed wide open, and *kept open* during the whole time of the exercises. If spectators come, and on their account windows and doors are closed, a positive injury is being done to the exercisers. Far better turn out the spectators than shut out God's pure air.

What a pitiable thing it is that our civilization can do no better for us than to make us slaves to indoor life, so that we have to go and take artificial exercise in order to preserve our health. Think of the vigor and strength, the robustness and power, the joy and the health, that are the possession of men and women of outdoor life. Let any one who wishes to know what this means read John Muir's *Mountains of California.* In it he tells of his years of experiences climbing the terribly difficult peaks of the Sierras, the exploring of glaciers, the sleeping out at night during snow-storms in the depth of winter without either an overcoat or a single blanket. One of the most thrilling of experiences is told as simply as the narrative of a child. He was out during a terrific wind-storm. Says he: "When the storm began to sound I lost no time in pushing out into the woods to enjoy it. For on such occasions Nature has always something rare to show us, and the danger to life and limb is hardly greater than one would experience crouching deprecatingly beneath a roof."

Think of a city-bred man, a society man, deliberately walking out into a storm to *enjoy* it.

"It was still early morning when I found myself fairly adrift. Delicious sunshine came pouring over the hills. . . . . I heard trees falling for hours at the rate of one every two or three minutes; some uprooted, partly on account of the loose, water-soaked condition of the ground; others broken straight across, where some weakness caused by fire had determined the spot. The gestures of the various trees made a delightful study. Young sugar-pines, light and feathery as squirrel-tails, were bowing almost to the ground; while the grand old patriarchs, whose massive boles had been tried in a hundred storms, waved solemnly above them, their long, arching branches streaming fluently on the gale, and every needle thrilling and singing and shedding off keen lances of light like a diamond.

"I drifted on through the midst of this passionate music and motion, across many a glen from ridge to ridge; often halting in the lee of a rock for shelter, or to gaze and listen. Even when the grand anthem had swelled to its highest pitch, I could distinctly hear the varying tones of individual trees,— spruce and fir and pine and leafless oak,— and even the infinitely gentle rustle of the withered grasses at my feet. Each was expressing itself in its own way, — singing its own song and making its own peculiar gestures, — manifesting a richness of variety to be found in no other forest I have yet seen.

"Toward midday, after a long, tingling scramble through copses of hazel and ceanothus, I gained the summit of the highest ridge in the neighborhood; and then it occurred to me that it would be a fine thing to climb one of the trees to obtain a wider outlook and get my ear close to the Æolian music of the topmost needles. But under the circumstances the choice of a tree was a serious matter. One whose instep was not very strong seemed in danger of being blown down, or of being struck by others in case they should fall; another was branchless to a considerable height above the ground, and at the same time too large to be grasped with arms and legs in climbing; while others were not favorably situated for clear views. After cautiously casting about, I made choice of the tallest of a group of Douglas spruces that were growing close together like a tuft of grass, no one of which seemed likely to fall unless all the rest fell with it. Though comparatively young, they were about 100 feet high, and their lithe, brushy tops were rocking and swirling in wild ecstasy. Being accustomed to climb trees in making botanical studies, I experienced no difficulty in reaching the top of this one, and never before did I enjoy so noble an exhilaration of motion. The slender tops fairly flapped and swished in the passionate torrent, bending and swirling backward and forward, round and round, tracing indescribable combinations of vertical and horizontal curves, while I clung with muscles firm braced, like a bobolink on a reed.

"In its wildest sweeps my tree-top described an arc of from twenty to thirty degrees, but I felt sure of its elastic temper, having seen others of the same species still more severely tried — bent almost to the ground, indeed, in heavy snows — without breaking a fiber. I was therefore safe, and free to take the wind into my pulses and enjoy the excited forest from my superb outlook. . . .

HAVASUPAI DRESSING BUCKSKIN.

"I kept my lofty perch for hours, frequently closing my eyes to enjoy the music by itself, or to feast quietly on the delicious fragrance that was streaming past."

What an experience, and what a joy to feel one's self able to enjoy it! I know what it is. Years before

I had read this, I had had a similar experience when driving over the high Sierras from the borders of Oregon, Nevada, and California down into southern California. Imagine the ordinary business man, or clerk, or banker, or preacher, or lawyer, or doctor, daring to climb so high a tree, and especially during such a storm. Yet such a day so spent is worth more than a year of any ordinary man's life.

Edward Robeson Taylor, the poet-mayor of San Francisco, once expressed his keen appreciation of what Nature gives to the man who loves her enough to test her. And he has made the test many a time, in the Sierras, in the forests, in the deserts, in the Grand Canyon, as well as on the Bay of San Francisco. He wrote:

> "In him that on the rugged breast of mountain
> Finds his joy and his repose,
> Who makes the pine his fellow, and with zest
> Treads the great glaciers and their kindred snows,
> A strength is planted that in direst test
> Dares all the devils of Danger to oppose."

Then, too, there are marvelous healing powers in God's great out-of-doors. The *vis medicatrix Naturæ* is no fiction of the imagination. If sick people knew enough, were wise enough, to go out into the open and discard all civilized modes of life, climbing mountains, sleeping on pine boughs, swimming in the streams, working in the soil, dabbling in the hot or cold springs, eating the ripe fruits and nuts, and bathing the whole body daily in bright sunshine, they would be brought to a health and vigor they had never before known.

I have often wondered why thoughtful white people have not observed that insanity is practically unknown amongst the Indians. Why? Our own great Emerson once wrote a clear answer.

"It was," said he, "the practice of the Orientals, especially of the Persians, to let insane persons wander at their own will out of the towns, into the desert, and, if they liked, to associate with wild animals. In their belief, wild beasts, especially gazelles, collect around an insane person, and live with him on a friendly footing. The patient found something curative in that intercourse, by which he was quieted and sometimes restored. But there are more insane persons than are called so, or are under treatment in hospitals. The crowd in the cities, at the hotels, theaters, card-tables, the speculators who rush for investment at ten per cent, twenty per cent, cent per cent, are all more or less mad — these point the moral, and persuade us to seek in the fields the health of the mind."

But not only does healing come to the *mind* in Nature: the diseased *soul* there finds medicine and health.

The well-beloved Robert Louis Stevenson was well aware of this out-of-door joy. Among many other fine things on the subject he once wrote the following which fully expresses my idea:

> "To wash in one of God's rivers in the open air seems to me a sort of cheerful solemnity or semi-pagan act of worship. To dabble among dishes in a bedroom may perhaps make clean the body; but the imagination takes no share in such a cleansing."

One of our great artists and writers, whose life went out a few years ago in sad eclipse, wrote with a clarity of vision that his awful experiences had taught him: "I have a strange longing for the great simple primeval things, such as the sea, to me no less of a mother than the earth. It seems to me that we all look at Nature too much, and live with her too little. I discern great sanity in the Greek attitude. They never chattered about sunsets, or discussed whether the shadows on the grass were really mauve or not. But they saw that the sea was for the swimmer, and the land for the feet of the runner. They loved the trees for the shadow

AN APACHE GRANDMOTHER AND SOME BASKETS OF HER OWN DESIGN AND WEAVE. ALL MADE IN THE OPEN AIR.

that they cast, and the forest for its silence at noon. The vineyard-dresser wreathed his hair with ivy, that he might keep off the rays of the sun as he stooped over the young shoots; and for the artist and the athlete, the two types that Greece gave us, they plaited with garlands the leaves of the bitter laurel and of the wild parsley, which else had been of no service to men.

. . . . I feel sure that in elemental forces there is purification, and I want to go back to them and live in their presence."

How literally true to fact is this assurance of purification out in the great elemental forces and places of Nature, and how the Indian daily demonstrates it. Thousands can testify to it. Here one becomes soothed. The grinning faces of hate do not pursue him here. Nature is passionless to the hunted man. She is willing to be wooed and won, and then opens up her rich treasures to the guiltiest and vilest of men, until they regain the right angle of vision, then the desire for purification, then repentance, then assurance of forgiveness, and finally their self-respect. Then they are able to return (if necessity compels) to civilization and bear any punishment that may be awarded, for in the rugged arms of Nature they have absorbed strength and power, — strength of will and power of soul to dare and do that which the highest within them compels.

Who that has read the *De Profundis* of that erratic and brilliant genius, Oscar Wilde, has not felt the sad pathos and yet intense truth of his concluding words? They are Indian-like in their direct truth and native strength.

"All trials are trials for one's life, just as all sentences are sentences of death; and three times I have been tried. The first time I left the box to be arrested, the second time to be led back to the house of detention, the third time to pass into a prison for two years. Society, as we have constituted it, will have no place for me, has none to offer; but Nature, whose sweet rains fall on unjust and just alike, will have clefts in the rocks where I may hide, and secret valleys in whose silence I may weep undisturbed. She will hang the night with stars so that I may walk abroad in the darkness without stumbling, and send the wind over my footprints so that none may track me to my hurt. She will cleanse me in great waters, and with bitter herbs make me whole."

This is one of the great wonders of the out-of-door life that the weary and sinful of the white race would do well to learn.

But not only does health of mind and soul return to the sinful in God's great out-of-doors: the most vigorous and pure, healthy and perfect, minds and souls are expanded and strengthened with such contact. Buddha, Mahomet, Moses, David, Elijah, Christ, were all lovers of out-of-doors. Washington, Lincoln, and Garfield were all out-of-door men. One learns in the solitude and primitive frankness of the free life of the out doors to do his own thinking, untrammeled by convention or prejudice. He sees things as they are. His soul is unclothed, and there can no longer be any deception or pretense. So he becomes an individual; not a mere rote thinker of other's thoughts, and not a mere parrot of other men's ideas. Edwin Markham could never have written *The Man with the Hoe* had he lived only in the city. He would never have seen deeply enough, and he would never have dared brave the conventional prejudices of the civilized (?) world as he did in his poem, had he been city-bred. But because he thought nakedly before God and his own soul he was compelled to see the monstrousness of making a man — a son of God, created in His image — a mere clod of clay. The idea that this poem is a reflection upon labor is utter nonsense. It is merely a protest, strong, vigorous, forceful as a thunder-storm, against compelling some men to labor so hard that they have neither time nor opportunity for mental and spiritual occupation, and have thus even lost the desire for or hope of gaining it. Labor is ennobling, but man is made for more than mere physical labor. The unequal distribution of affairs in this life causes some men to have no physical labor, to their vast disadvantage, while others have nothing but physical labor, equally to their disadvantage. The finding of a just equilibrium between these two extremes, and then aiding the men of both extremes to see the need of each helping the other, or of taking some of the burden of the other, would result in the immediate benefiting of the race to an incalculable extent, both in body, mind, and soul. And it is this for which I plead, earnestly calling upon my fellows to so adjust their own lives that they will strike the happy mean, thus *living* (not merely talking about) the dignity of labor as well as the joy of mental and spiritual occupation.

Another important thing must not be overlooked. As a result of this out-of-door life the Indian is an early riser and an early retirer to bed. The civilized habit of turning night into day, living in the glare of gas and electric light, is, on the face of it, artificial, unnatural, and unhealthful. It is indefensible from every standpoint. There is not one word of good can be said of it. The day is made for work, the night for rest and sleep. The use of artificial light to the extent we indulge it in civilization is gradually rendering normal eyesight a rarity. Children are born with myoptic and other eye-diseased tendencies. Sometimes it seems as if more people, of all ages, wear glasses than use their natural eyesight, and this is but one of many sad consequences accruing in part from our reversal of the natural use of the day and night times.

Many men, literary and others, wait until the quiet of evening to do their work. They often stimulate themselves with coffee, and even stronger beverages, and then work until the "wee sma' hours," by arti-

HAPPY AND HEALTHY HOPI CHILDREN, ASKING THE AUTHOR FOR CANDY.

ficial light, *after they have already done a fair day's work.* We used to hear a great many words of commendation of the youths in school and college who "burned the midnight oil." If I had my way I would "use the leather strap" upon all these burners-up of their physical and mental forces at the time God intended they should be abed and asleep. The time for mental work is in the early morning after a hearty, healthy, good night's sleep. The body is strengthened, the mind refreshed, and thought flows easily and readily, because all weariness has disappeared under the influence of "tired nature's sweet restorer." Mental work done at such time is not only a pleasure, but is well done, properly done, because the conditions are right for its doing.

Nor is this all. There is a mental and spiritual pleasure given to the early riser that the late sleeper knows nothing of. One of the most beautiful baskets in my historic collection of Indian baskets is one made by a Coahuila woman who depicted thereon the white light of the morning shining through the dark silhouettes of the sharp points of the giant cactus. Her æsthetic enjoyment was thus made the inspiration of a real work of art.

How much white people lose by not seeing and knowing the beauty of the early morning hours,— the hours just preceding dawn, and during the first outburst of the sun! A friend and I stood out the other morning before sunrise, looking at the exquisite delicate lights over the mountain peaks, and she gave expression to the above thought, and only a few days before I had said it to a friend as we had wended our way from *El Tovar* Hotel at the Grand Canyon out to O'Neill Point to see the sunrise. Elisha Safford eloquently speaks as follows of this:

BEAUTY OF THE MORNING

Oh, the beauty of the morning! It showers its splendors down
From the crimson robes of sunrise, the azure mountain's crown;
It smiles amid the waving fields, it dapples in the streams,
It breathes its sparkling music through the rapture of our dreams.

It floats upon the limpid air in rainbow clouds of mist,
It ripples through the glowing skies in pearl and amethyst,
It gleams in every burnished pool, it riots through the grass,
It splashes waves of glory on the shadows as they pass.

It steals among the nodding trees and to the forest croons,
In airy note and gentle voice, 'neath waning plenilunes;
It calls, and lo! the wooded brakes, the hills and tangled fens —
A world of life and mystery — swarm with its denizens.

It trembles in the perfumed breeze, and where its ardor runs,
A thousand light-winged choristers pant forth their orisons;
A thousand echoes clap their hands, and from their dewy beds,
A million scarlet-throated flowers peer forth with startled heads.

Oh, the beauty of the morning! It rains upon our ears:
The music of the universe, the chiming of the spheres;
From cloistered wood and leafy vale, its tuneful medleys throng,
Till all the earth is drenched in light and all the world in song!

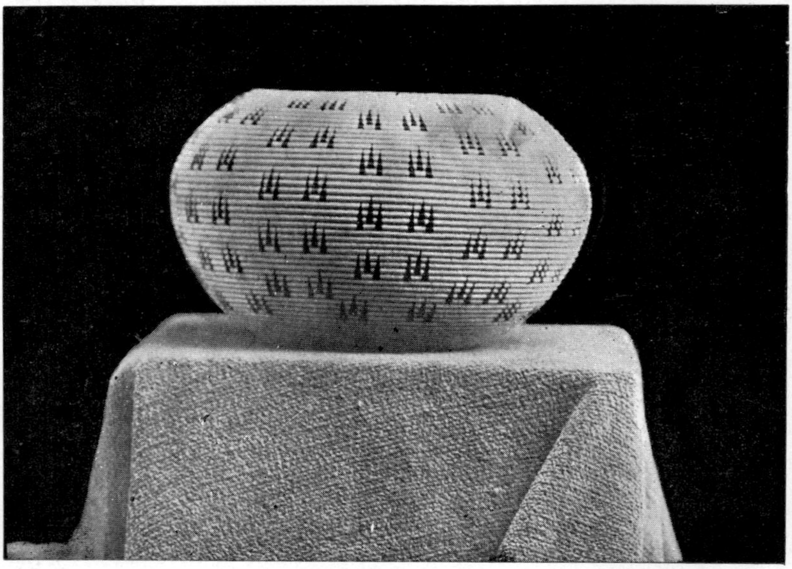

INDIAN BASKET, SHOWING INFLUENCE OF NATURE IN THE DESIGN.

THE INDIAN AND OUT-OF-DOOR LIFE

All children, and especially city children, need out-of-door life. Men and women need it too, sadly, but if the elders cannot have it, owing to our perverted social conditions, our law-givers should see to it that the children do better. It is a well-known fact that cities would soon die out if their vast populations were not constantly being replenished by the sons and daughters of the country. So instead of letting our city children grow up to imperfect manhood, let us find some way to get them out of doors and out into the country more and more. Exercise in the open, where pure air penetrates to the full depths of the lungs, personal contact with the soil, and physical work upon it, as well as personal contact with the trees and flowers and all growing things, the animals of the farm and field, the rocks and mountains, the hills and valleys, the waterfalls and streams, the deserts and canyons; all these are to be desired. Who does not wish to sing with Edwin Markham:

> "I ride on the mountain tops, I ride,
> I have found my life and am satisfied!"

Of course this out-in-the-country life for city children can only be gained if their parents and our educators and politicians combine to provide it. And in some way it ought to be done. What a joy it would be to many a city boy to be allowed to go and do some work in the country during certain times in the year! Those who have seen the city children who are taken yearly into the country by Fresh Air Funds, or out by vessel into the Bay of New York or Boston Harbor, by philanthropic people, know what delight, joy, and health they receive from the outing. These things all point to the great, the dire, the awful need there is for some way of giving to our city children and men and women more out-door life.

Just after the San Francisco earthquake, Dr. J. H. Kellogg, editor of *Good Health*, wrote in his forceful way of some lessons the people might learn from that disaster. Here is one of them bearing upon this very question:

MONO INDIAN COOKING CORN MUSH IN A BASKET BY A CAMP FIRE.

"Three hundred thousand people have found out that they can live out of doors, and that out of doors is a safer place than indoors.

"People who have all their lives slept on beds of down, protected by thick walls of brick or stone, barricaded against the dangerous (?) air of night, have found that it is possible to spend a night upon an unsheltered hillside without risk to life, and it is more than likely that, as in the case of the Charleston earthquake, not a few modern troglodytes, who scarcely ever saw the light of day before, have been actually benefited by being forced out into the fresh air and the sunshine.

"The great tent colonies, improvised by the military

authorities with such promptness under the efficient management of the able General Funston, may become the permanent homes for some of the thousands who are now for the first time in their lives tasting the sweets of an out-of-door life. Man is an out-of-door creature, meant to live amid umbrageous freshness, his skin bathed clean by morning dews or evening showers, browned and disinfected by the sun, fed by tropic fruits, and cheered by tropic birds and flowers. It is only through long generations of living under artificial conditions that civilized man has become accustomed to the unhealthful and disease-producing influences of the modern house to such a degree that they can be even in a small measure tolerated. But this immunity is only apparent. An atmosphere that will kill a Hottentot or a baboon in six months will also kill a bank president or a trust magnate — *sometime.* And if these tent-dwellers get such a taste of the substantial advantages of the out-of-door life that they refuse to return to the old unwholesome conditions of anti-earthquake days, they will profit substantially by their experience, terrible though it has been. It takes earthquakes and cyclones and tidal waves to jostle us out of the unnatural and degenerative ruts into which conventionality is always driving us.

"What advantages has the man in the brown-stone front over the man in the tent? Only these: A pale face instead of the brown skin which is natural to his species; a coated tongue, no appetite, and no digestion, instead of the keen zest for food and splendid digestive vigor of the tent-dweller; an aching head and confused mind and depressed spirits, instead of the vim and snap and energy, mental and physical, and the freedom from pain and pessimism of out-of-door dwellers;

early consumption or apoplexy or paresis or cancer of the stomach or arteriosclerosis, — the dry rot of the body which stealthily weakens the props and crumbles the foundations of the citadel of life."

Why is it that in our cities in summer, and in Florida and the South generally, and in the West, we do not follow the French custom of eating out of doors?

American visitors to Paris in the summer time have always been impressed by the prevalent custom there of dining out of doors. The sidewalks in front of cafés and restaurants are always so occupied with chairs and tables that pedestrians often have to step into the street to get by. This has long been the summer custom in Paris, but with the arrival of cold weather tables and chairs disappeared every year, and the diners returned to the close nicotine-laden air of the stuffy little dining-rooms inside. But last year, according to the London correspondent of the *Outlook*, an enterprising Frenchman, finding his patrons much attached to his open-air dining-room, and being short of room inside, undertook to make his guests comfortable out of doors by means of a large brazier placed upon the sidewalk. Others followed his example, and in a short time the streets were lined with braziers from the Madeline to the Bastile, much to the satisfaction of the cab-drivers and newsboys. One ingenious proprietor made his table-legs hollow, filled with hot water, and thus utilized them as foot-warmers. And so one may now enjoy a fashionable Parisian café *au plein air* any day in the year.

Everybody is always hungry at a picnic, not simply because of the unusual exercise, but as the result of the tonic appetite-stimulating influence of the out-of-doors.

The same plan may be introduced into any private home by utilizing a back porch, or, when this is lacking, a tent-cloth awning may be provided at the expense of a few dollars.

The old Spanish *patio*, or inner court, provided the seclusion that many desire, with the possibility of a larger out-of-door life. Mr. Gustav Stickley, the far-seeing editor of *The Craftsman*, which so effectually pleads for a simpler and more democratic life for the people, has planned a number of *Craftsman* houses in which these open porches for eating, and sleeping as well, are introduced. This is a great step in the right direction, and is strongly to be commended.

But the outdoor life is larger than houses and porches. One must get away from all houses to really feel and know the joy of the great out-of-doors. Every teacher and orator should know the birds and trees, the flowers and grasses, the rocks and stars, the clouds and odors, *at first hand.* He should not depend upon books at all for any of this knowledge, save as guides to obtain it. Instead of reading books he should read Nature. See how powerful is the simple oratory of the Indian, whose figures and similes and illustrations and metaphors are of those things in Nature with which he is perfectly familiar.

Another effect upon the mind and soul as the result of this outdoor life is remarkable to those who have never given it a thought. One of our poets once said, "The undevout astronomer is mad." And every Indian will tell you that the undevout Indian is either mad or "getting civilized." One of our California historians once wrote something to the effect that the California Indian had no religion, no mythology, no reverence, no belief in anything outside of and beyond himself. Jeremiah Curtin, a careful and close student of the California Indian for many years, in his wonderfully interesting book, "Creation Myths of Primitive America," shows the utter fallacy of this idea. He says: "Primitive man in America stood at every step face to face with divinity as he knew or understood it. He could never escape from the presence of those powers which had constituted the first world, and which composed all that there was in the present one. . . . . The most important question of all in Indian life was communication with divinity, intercourse with the spirits of divine personages." Indeed, the Indian sees the divine power in everything. His God speaks in the storm, the howling wind, the tornado, the hurricane, the roaring rapids and dashing cataracts of the rivers, the never-ending rise and fall of the ocean, the towering mountains and the tiny hills, the trees, the bees, the buds and blossoms. It is God in the flower that makes it grow and gives it its odor; that makes the tree from the acorn; that makes the sun to shine; that sends the rain and dew and the gentle zephyrs. The thunder is His voice, and everything in Nature is an expression of His thought.

This belief compels the Indian to a close study of Nature. Hence the keenness of his powers of observation. He knows every plant, and when and where it best grows. He knows the track of every bird, insect reptile, and animal. He knows all the signs of the weather. He is a past-master in woodcraft, and knows more of the habits of plants and animal life than all of our trained naturalists put together. He is a poet, too, withal, and an orator, using the knowledge he has of nature in his thought and speech. No writer that ever lived knew the real Indian so well as

Fenimore Cooper, and we all know the dignified and poetical speech of his Indian characters. I know scores and hundreds of dusky-skinned Henry D. Thoreaus and John Burroughses, John Muirs and Elizabeth Grinnells and Olive Thorne Millers. Indeed, to get an Indian once started upon his lore of plant, tree, insect, bird, or animal, is to open up a flood-gate which will deluge any but the one who knows what to expect.

CHAPTER V

THE INDIAN AND SLEEPING OUT OF DOORS

AS I have already intimated, the Indian is practically an out-of-door sleeper. I say "practically," for there are exceptions to the general rule. The

TERRACED HOUSES OF THE HOPIS, ALLOWING SLEEPING OUT OF DOORS.

Hopis of northern Arizona have houses. In the cold winter months they sleep indoors whenever they can. The Navahos, Apaches, Havasupais, and other tribes have their "hogans" and "hawas" in which they sleep in the very cold weather. But in the summer the invariable rule is for all to sleep out of doors. And even in the winter, if duty calls them away from home and they have to camp out, they sleep in the cold, on the snow, in the rain, as unconcerned for their health as if they were well protected indoors. It is this latter feature that so much commends itself to me. It is just as *natural* to them to have to sleep out of doors as it is to sleep indoors. They think no more of it, do not regard it as an unusual and dangerous experience, or one to be dreaded. They accept it without a murmur or complaint, and without fear. This is an attitude of mind that I would the white race would learn from the Indian. I once had a friend, a city-bred man, born and brought up in New York, sent west to me by his physician because he had had two or three hemorrhages, whom I took out into Arizona. The first night we had to sleep out was very cold, for it was early in the year, and at that high altitude the thermometer sank very rapidly after the sun went down. Yet I deliberately called camp by the side of a great snowbank. The fearful invalid wanted to know what I was stopping there for. I told him it was to afford him a good sleeping place on the snow. He expressed his dread, and assured me that such an experience would kill him at once. I told him that if it did I would see that he was decently buried, but that did not seem to dissipate his fears. After a good camp-fire was built, and he had had a warm and comforting supper, and his blankets were stretched out on the snow, and he was undressed and well wrapped up, with a hot rock at his feet and the cheery blaze lighting up the scene, he felt less alarmed. I talked him to sleep, and when he awoke in the morning it was to confess that his throat and lungs felt more comfortable than they had done for many long months. A month of this open-air sleeping gave him new ideas on the subject, and sent him back east to fit up a camp in the Adirondacks, where he could get a

BOSTON MILLIONAIRES SLEEPING OUT OF DOORS ON THE SANDS OF THE COLORADO RIVER.

great deal of outdoor life, and sleeping with doors and windows wide open.

The outdoor treatment for tuberculosis is now almost universal. Here is what one eminent authority says on the subject:

"Tuberculosis is a direct result of over-work, either mental or physical, and rest is largely its cure.

This life in the open air is best carried out in a sitting or semi-reclining posture. Every hour of the day in all seasons of the year and in all kinds of weather should thus be spent, together with sleeping in a tent, protected veranda, or in a house with windows wide open. It will be found that the colder the weather, the more marked and permanent the results. One does not need to be uncomfortable; one can be well wrapped with heavy blankets. It is the inhalation of cold air that is so effectual in stimulating appetite, as a general tonic and fever reducer. A consumptive should have for his motto: 'Every hour in the closed house is an hour lost.' There is no excuse for losing time."

But it is not for those who are in ill health alone that I would commend out-of-door sleeping. Those who are healthy need to be kept in health, and there is a vim, a vigor, a physical joy, comes from this habit that I would that every child, young man and woman, and adult in the land might enjoy. Here is what one intelligent writer, Mary Heath, has recently said upon this subject, and her words I most heartily indorse:

"The success of any scheme for human betterment, morally, mentally, or physically, depends upon securing human co-operation by convincing the intellect of the truth or falsity of any widespread belief. The almost universal notion that night air is dangerous has predisposed, more than any other one cause, to the shutting of every door and window at sunset to keep out malaria. Notwithstanding the fact that all air analyses show that outdoor night air is much purer than day air, the old fear of night air still remains, and is responsible for much infection from foul air, because outdoor and indoor workers in summer and winter — all alike — spend their sleeping hours in ill-ventilated bedrooms. After false ideas about the harmfulness of fresh air are eradicated, plans should be devised and utilized for arranging outdoor sleeping apartments; plans should also be devised for keeping the body warm in cold weather without an over-amount of bedclothing; and for the health and convenience of the millions of middle class and more or less humble domestic home workers, provisions should be made for doing the housework as much as possible out of doors, away from the kitchen heat and odors of cooking food. Out-of-door recreation for the family should also be provided for. Could all sedentary workers spend the seven to nine hours of sleep in a clean, outdoor atmosphere, many of the evil effects of indoor sedentary work would be neutralized. The shop, office, or factory employe, after sleeping in the pure night air, would awake invigorated for the day's demands and duties. Beginning the day aright, with a keen normal appetite for healthful food, he would be able to utilize his working energies without either structural damage to the tissues, or intellectual or moral degradation."

Elbert Hubbard, of Roycroft fame, has converted all the sleeping-rooms of his phalanstery into outdoor rooms, where fresh, pure air is breathed. Dr. Kellogg, editor of *Good Health*, sleeps out of doors all the time, and all his large family of adopted children have rooms which practically contain no doors or windows, so that they sleep as near the open air as civilization will allow.

For years, as far as was possible, I have slept out of doors. When at home my bed is on an open porch, my face turned to the stars, the waving of plum, peach, and fig trees making music while I sleep, the beautiful lights of earliest dawn cheering my eyes before I arise, and the twittering and singing of the birds putting melodies into my soul as I dress. When I am in the wilds exploring, I sleep out of doors always, when and where I can. Those who have read my various books know of my experiences of sleeping in storms, during heavy rains, without bedding in rocky washes, in leaky boats and the rain pouring upon us, in the heat of the desert, and the cold of the snowy plateaus of Arizona. Yet I do not remember that I ever once "took cold," though I have been wet through many a night. On the other hand, I never visit civilization, especially the proud, haughty, conceited civilization of the East, where houses are steam-heated, and street and railway cars are superheated, without taking severe colds and suffering much misery.

Those who have heard Nansen and Peary and other arctic explorers will remember that they had the same experience. Is it not apparent, therefore, that the outdoor life is the normal, the healthful, the rational, the *natural* life, while that of the steam-heated house is abnormal, unhealthful, irrational, and unnatural?

People often say: But I see that my house is well ventilated, and therefore the air is as pure and good as it is out of doors. In reply, permit me to say that no house can ever be well ventilated. Air to be pure and wholesome must be *alive.* It can only live when free and uncontained, and in contact with the direct rays of the sun during the day. Every thoughtful person has noticed the great difference there is between outdoor air and indoor air, on stepping from outside inside, even through all the doors and windows of the room were wide open. There is a vast difference between indoor and outdoor air, even under the best of conditions; so get into the open all you can, day or night, winter or summer, wet or dry.

One of the finest and strongest poems in the language is the following, by Richard Burton:

GOD'S GIFT, THE AIR

Now, is there anything that freer seems
  Than air, the fresh, the vital, that a man
Draws in with breathings bountiful, nor dreams
  Of any better bliss, because he can
Make over all his blood thereby, and feel
Once more his youth return, his muscles steel,
  And life grow buoyant, part of God's good plan!

Oh, how on plain and mountain, and by streams
  That shine along their path; o'er many a field
Proud with pied flowers, or where sunrise gleams
  In spangled splendors, does the rich air yield
Its balsam; yea, how hunter, pioneer,
Lover, and bard have felt that heaven was near
  Because the air their spirit touched and healed!

And yet — God of the open! — look and see
  The millions of thy creatures pent within
Close places that are foul for one clean breath,
Thrilling with health, and hope, and purity;
  Nature's vast antidote for stain and sin,
Life's sweetest medicine this side of death!
How comes it that this largess of the sky
Thy children lack of, till they droop and die?

Many white people go out tenting in the summer and think they are sleeping out of doors. What a foolish error. Here is what a scientific authority says upon the subject:

"Are you tenting? If so, you should know:

"That a well-closed tent is nearly air-tight, and consequently,—

"That in an ordinary-sized tent, one occupant will

A CHEMEHUEVI INDIAN AND HIS OUT-OF-DOOR SHELTER FROM THE SUN.

so pollute the air as to render it unfit to breathe in less than twenty minutes; two occupants, in less than ten minutes.

"That if you are tenting for your health, an opening at each end of the tent must be provided for ventilation at night. The openings should be at least a foot square for each occupant.

"Breathing impure air lowers the vitality, and consequently renders one susceptible to colds and other diseased conditions."

CHAPTER VI

THE INDIAN AS A WALKER, RIDER, AND CLIMBER

AS a part of his out-of-door life the Indian is a great walker and runner, having horses he is a great rider, and living in a mountainous or canyon region he is a great climber. The Indian walks through necessity, and also through delight and joy. He knows to the full "the joy of mere living." A few miles' walk, more or less, is nothing to him, and he does it so easily that one can see he enjoys it. In one of my books* I tell the story of the running powers of the Hopi Indians of northern Arizona. It is worth quoting here:

"It is no uncommon thing for an Oraibi or Mashonganavi to run from his home to Moenkopi, a distance of forty miles, over the hot blazing sands of a real American Sahara, there hoe his corn-field, and return to his home, within twenty-four hours. I once photographed, the morning after his return, an old man who had made this eighty-mile run, and he showed not the slightest trace of fatigue.

"For a dollar I have several times engaged a young man to take a message from Oraibi to Keam's Canyon, a distance of seventy-two miles, and he has run on foot the whole distance, delivered his message, and brought me an answer within thirty-six hours.

"One Oraibi, Ku-wa-wen-ti-wa, ran from Oraibi

*The Indians of the Painted Desert Region. Little, Brown & Co., Boston, illustrated, $2.00 net, 20c postage.

to Moenkopi, thence to Walpi, and back to Oraibi, a distance of over ninety miles, in one day."

I doubt not that most of my readers suppose that these experiences are rare and unusual, and come after special training. Not at all! They are regular occurrences, made without any thought that the white man was either watching or recording. When asked for the facts, the Indians gave them as simply and as unconcernedly as we might tell of a friend met or a dinner eaten. And it is not with one tribe alone. I have found the same endurance with Yumas, Pimas, Apaches, Navahos, Havasupais, Wallapais, Chemehuevis, Utes, Paiutis, and Mohaves. Indeed, on the trackless wastes of the Colorado desert the Mohaves and Yumas perhaps show a greater endurance than any people I have ever seen.

As a horseback-rider the Indian can teach many things to the white race. Among the Navahos and Hopis, the Havasupais and Wallapais, the Pimas and Apaches, most of the children are taught to ride at an early age. They can catch, bridle, and saddle their own horses while they are still "little tots," and the way they ride is almost a marvel. There need be no wonder at this, for their mothers are as used to horseback-riding as they are. Many an Indian child has come near to being born on horseback. They ride up and down trails, over the plains and up the mountains. They go with their parents gathering the seeds and pinion nuts, and are also taught to handle their horses in the chase. They study "horse-nature," and early become expert horse-breakers. While their animals are broncos and wild, and therefore are never as well "broken" as are ours, they compel them to every duty, and ride them fearlessly and constantly.

The girls and women, too, ride almost as much as the boys and men, and *always astride.* If anything were needed to demonstrate to an Indian woman the inferiority of a white woman it would be that she sits on a side-saddle. The utter unnaturalness and folly of such a posture is so incomprehensible to the Indian mind that she "throws up her hands," figuratively speaking, and gives up the problem of solving the peculiar mentality of her white sister. And I don't wonder! Thank God the day is passing when women are ashamed of having legs, or of placing one of them on one side and the other on the other side of a horse. Common sense and comfort will ultimately prevail, and place the most modest, refined, cultured, and womenly women upon the backs of their horses cavalier fashion, dressed in trousers. The idea that men should dictate to women what they should do to be womanly is so absurd as to make even fools laugh. What does a man know as to what is womanly? Women alone can determine that question, just as men alone must determine what is manly. So I am satisfied that I shall live to see womenly women — the best the world has — reasonably *natural* in their dress on horseback, and riding as the Creator evidently intended them to do.

If girls as well as boys of the white race were to ride horseback more, much disease would flee away. Liver and stomach troubles are shaken out of existence on horseback; the blue devils and constipation are almost an impossibility, and the exhilaration of the swift motion and the vivifying influence of the deeper breathing, the shaking up of the muscles and nerves, the quickening effect of the accelerated heart action, and the readier circulation of well-oxygenated blood

A ZUNI INDIAN WITH A JAR OF WATER UPON HER HEAD.

make the whole body a-tingle with a newness of life that is glorious. If I were well to do and had a score of children their chief education should be out of doors, and rain or shine, storm or calm, snow or sleet, winter or summer, boys and girls alike should ride horseback ten to twenty miles or more each day.

Nor should this do away with daily walking. Walking is a fine offset to riding. One needs to walk a good deal to enjoy riding a good deal. One is a necessary complement to the other. One exercise uses muscles that are little called upon by the other. So I would make good walkers, in all weathers, of all boys, girls, men, and women of the white race, even as are those of the Indian race. In order to be good walkers the Indians have naturally found the most perfect and natural attitude for walking. Every Indian walks upright, his abdomen in, chest up, chin down, and spinal column easily carrying his body and arms. The white race may well learn from the Indian how to keep the spinal column upright, how to have a graceful carriage in walking, and how to cure stooped shoulders. With all younger women and men of all ages among the Indians a curved spine, ungraceful walk, and stooped shoulders are practically unknown. The women produce this result by carrying burdens upon their heads.

Yes, and the boys and men as well carry burdens also upon the head, though not as much as the women. Burden carrying upon the head is a good thing. As one writer has well said:

"Most of us are accustomed to regard the head as a mere thinking machine, unconscious of the fact that this bony superstructure seems to have been specially adapted by Nature to the carrying of heavy weights.

"The arms are usually considered as the means intended for the bearing of burdens, but the effect of carrying heavy articles in the hands or on the arms is very injurious, and altogether destructive of an erect or graceful carriage. The shoulders are dragged forward, the back loses its natural curve, the lungs are compressed, and internal organs displaced.

"When the head bears the weight of the burden, as it is made to do among the peasant women of Italy, Mexico, and Spain, and the people of the Far East, there is great gain in both health and beauty. The muscles of the neck are strengthened, the spine held erect, the chest raised and expanded, so that breathing is full and deep, and the shoulders are held back in their natural position.

"It is a good thing for children to be early accustomed to the carrying of various articles, gradually

A YOKUT INDIAN WITH A WHEELBARROW LOAD OF PEACHES AND FIGS. THE CARRYING BASKET IS SUSPENDED BY A BROAD BAND OVER THE FOREHEAD.

increasing in weight, balanced upon the head. In this way they may acquire an erect carriage, and free and graceful walk."

THE INDIAN AS A WALKER

The Indian man and woman will pick up an olla of water, containing a gallon or more, and swinging it easily to the top of the head will walk along with hands by their sides, as unconcernedly as if they carried no fragile bowl balanced and ready to fall at the slightest provocation. And they will climb up steep and difficult trails, still balancing the jar upon the head. The effect of this is to compel a natural and dignified carriage. I know Navaho, Hopi, and Havasupai women who walk with a simple dignity that is not surpassed in drawing-room of president or king.

Then, too, another reason for this dignified, healthfully erect carriage is found in the fact that neither men nor women wear high-heeled shoes. The moccasin is always flat, and therefore the foot of the Indian rests firmly and securely upon the floor. No doubt if the Indian woman wished to imitate the forward motion of the kangaroo, or any other frivolous creature, she could tilt herself in an unnatural and absurd position by high-heeled shoes, but in all my twenty-five years of association with them I never found one foolish enough to do so.

The men, as well as the women, gain this upright attitude as the result of "holding up their vital organs" when they go for their long hunting and other tramps. It seems to me that fully one-half the white men (and women) we meet on the streets are suffering from prolapsus of the transverse colon. This is evidenced by the projection of the abdomen, which generally grows larger as they grow older; so that we have "tailors for fat men," and special implements of torture for compressing into what we call a decent shape the *embonpoint* of women. But, I ask, as I see the Indians, *why do white people have this paunch?*

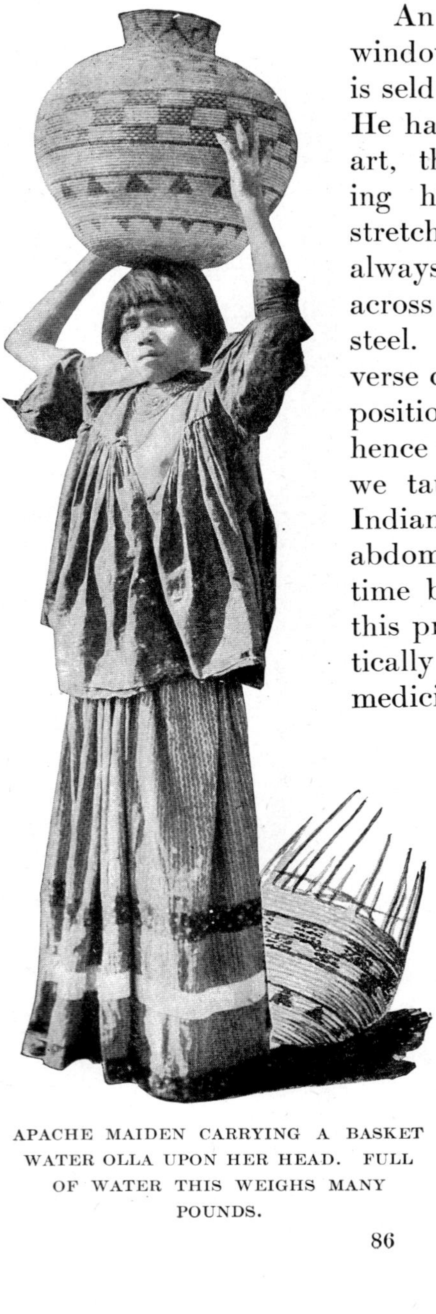

APACHE MAIDEN CARRYING A BASKET WATER OLLA UPON HER HEAD. FULL OF WATER THIS WEIGHS MANY POUNDS.

An Indian with a "bay-window" stomach, a paunch, is seldom, if ever seen. Why? He has long ago learned the art, the necessity, of keeping his abdominal muscles stretched tight. His belly is always held in. The muscles across his abdomen are like steel. The result is the transverse colon is held securely in position. It has no prolapse, hence there is no paunch. If we taught ourselves, as the Indian does, to draw in the abdomen and at the same time breathe long and deep, this prolapsus would be practically impossible. Half the medicine that is sold to so-called "kidney sufferers" is sold to people whose kidneys are no more diseased than are those of the man in the moon. It is the pulling and tugging of the falling colon that causes the wearisome backache; and the lying and scoundrelous wretches who prey upon the ignorant write out their catch-penny advertisements describing these feelings, so that when the sufferer picks up their literature he is as good as entrapped for "a dozen or more bottles," or until his money gives out.

O men and women of America, learn to walk upright, as God intended you should. Do not become "chesty" by throwing out your chest, and throwing your shoulders back at the expense of your spine, but pull in the muscles of your abdomen, fill your lungs with air, then pull your chin down and in, and you will soon have three great, grand, and glorious blessings; viz., a dignified, upright carriage; freedom from and reasonable assurance that you will never have prolapsus of the transverse colon and its attendant miseries and backache; and a lung capacity that will help you withstand the approaches of disease should you ever, in some other way, come under its malign influence.

When I see white boys slouching and shambling along the streets I wish with a great wish that I could have them put under the training of some of my wild Indian friends. They would soon brace up; heads would be held erect, chins down, abdomen in, chest up, and with lips closed, and the pure air of the mountain, canyon, plain, desert, or forest entering their lungs through the nostrils; the whole aspect of life would begin to change. For "nothing lifts up the spirits so much as just to lift the chest up. It takes a load off the head, off the mind, off the heart. Raise your chest so high that the abdominal organs perform their functions in a proper way. When one is all doubled over, the head and spine are deprived of blood that they are entitled to. When the chest is lifted up, the abdominal organs are compressed, and the blood that has been retired from the circulation and accu-

HAVASUPAI CHILD WITH WATER BOTTLE SUSPENDED FROM THE FOREHEAD.

mulated in the liver and the stomach is forced back into the current where it belongs. The head and spinal cord get their proper supply of blood, and one feels refreshed and energized immediately."

But in addition to their walking and riding the Indians are great climbers of steep canyon and mountain trails. Men, women, and children alike pass up and down these trails with almost the ease and agility of the goat. I have seen a woman with a *kathak* (carrying basket) suspended from her forehead containing a load of fruit, of pine nuts, of grass seeds, weighing not less than from 50 to 100 lbs., her baby perched on top of the load, steadily and easily climb a trail that made me puff and blow like a grampus. Few exercises, properly taken, are of greater benefit to the lungs and heart, and indeed, all the vital organs, than is trail or mountain climbing. See that your clothing is easy, especially around the waist, for there must be room for every effort of lung expansion. This applies to men as well as to women, for the wretched and injurious habit is growing among men of wearing a belt instead of suspenders. If the prospective climber is a woman, let her wear a loose, light dress, and with as short a skirt as her common sense, judgment, and conscience will allow her to wear. If she is out "in the wilds," let her wear trousers and discard skirts entirely as a senseless and barbarous slavery to custom and convention. Shoes should be easy and comfortable, with thick soles and broad, *low* heels.

Begin to climb as early in the morning as possible. Don't try to do too much at first. Try a small hill. Conquer that by degrees. Get so that you can finally go up and down without any great effort. Then tackle the higher hills, and finally try real mountains, eight,

CLIMBING THE TRAILS IN THE CANYON OF THE HAVASU, ARIZONA.

ten, fourteen thousand feet high. If you are delicate to begin with be more careful still, and ask the advice of your physician, but don't be afraid so long as you do not get fatigued to exhaustion. For climbing develops the thighs and calves of the leg, the muscles of the back, enlarges the lungs, makes the heart pump more and purer (because better oxygenated) blood throughout the whole body, brings about more rapid changes in the material of the body, and thus exchanges old and useless tissue for new and healthy, dissolves and dissipates fat, induces perspiration and exhalations through the kidneys that are peculiarly beneficial.

In breathing be sure to keep the mouth closed. Insist upon *nasal* breathing, and the exercise will perforce make it *deep* breathing. The deeper you breathe the more good you will get from it. Let the posture be correct or you will lose much good. This is in brief: pull the abdomen in, raise the chest, keep the chin down, and let the arms hang easily and naturally by the side.

For years I have compelled myself to seize every possible opportunity for trail climbing or descending. Hundreds of miles of trails have I gone up and down in the Grand Canyon of Arizona, often with a thirty, forty, fifty pound camera and food supplies on my back. I have ascended scores of mountains throughout the Southwest, and the rich experiences of glowing health and vigor, vim, snap, tingle, that come from such exercises no one can know but those who have enjoyed them.

A few weeks ago I came to the Grand Canyon (September, 1907), after nearly a year of rest from physical labor on an extended scale (my civilized occupations had pre-empted all my time). I started out on the trail, up and down Havasu Canyon, Bass Trail of the Grand Canyon, and the Grand View and Red Canyon trails. Again and again I walked up the steepest portions for a mile at a time, setting the pace for the horses and mules, and it was a source of mental as well as physical delight that my lungs, heart, and body generally were in such good condition that I could do this day after day for two weeks, not only without exhaustion, but with positive exhilaration and physical delight.

CHAPTER VII

THE INDIAN IN THE RAIN AND THE DIRT

HOW these "things we may learn from the Indian" grow upon us, as we study the "noble red man" in his own haunts. Again and again I have noticed that "*he doesn't know enough to go in when it rains.*" The white man who first coined that expression deemed it an evidence of smartness, and reared his head more proudly than his fellows because he was the author of so bright an idea. Yet when you come to consider it, what a foolish proposition it is! Go in when it rains? Why should you go in? Do the birds go in? I have just been watching them from my study window,— larks, linnets, song-sparrows, and mocking-birds. Not one of them seems to care a particle about the rain, and their songs are as sweet and as cheery and as full of melody as they are on the days of brightest sunshine. How well I recall seeing a mocking-bird on a stand on my lawn one day when the rain was pouring down fiercely. He stood with bill up and tail down so that he had a very "Gothic-roof-like" appearance, his mouth wide open, and as the rain poured from the end of his tail he sent out a flood of melody more rich and sweet than any bird-song I ever heard.

And the horses! How they enjoy the rain! I have seen them loose in a stable having double doors, the upper of which was open, and when it rained they would thrust their noses out into the rain and let the drippings of the eaves fall upon them with evident pleasure and longing that they might get out into it all over.

Nothing alive in Nature save "civilized" man dreads the rain. The Indian fairly revels in it. I was once at the Havasupai village for a couple of weeks, the guest of my friend Wa-lu-tha-ma. His little girl, seven years old, was a perfect little witch. She was

HEALTHY NAVAHO CHILDREN USED TO THE RAIN AND THE OUT OF DOORS.

quick, nervy, lively, and healthy. When it rained and her clothes got wet I tried to prevail upon her to come into shelter. But no! She wanted to be out in the rain, and off she sprang through the door, playing with the pools as they collected, and running with others of her playmates to where the extemporized waterfalls dashed themselves into semi-spray as they fell from the heights above upon the shelving rocks. Here they stood, in the water and rain, like dusky fairies, laughing and shouting, romping and sporting, in perfect glee.

The older women, too, mind it but little, unless it is very cold or the wind is blowing. They no more mind being wet than they do that the wind should blow or the sun shine, and as for any ill effect that either children or grown-ups suffer from the wet, I have yet to see it. Why? The reasons are clear. In the first place, they have no fear of the rain. It is not constantly instilled into their minds from childhood that "they mustn't get wet, or they'll take cold," and girls are not taught to expect functional disarrangement if they "get their feet wet." This has something to do with it, for the effect of the mind upon the body is far more potent than we yet know.

In the second place, they move about with natural activity in the rain as at other times. This keeps the blood circulating and prevents any lowering of the temperature of the body.

In the third place, their general out-of-door life gives them such a robustness that if there is any tax upon the system it is fully ready to meet it.

But I am asked, "Would you advocate white people, especially girls and women, getting wet? Think of their skirts bedraggled in the rain, and how these

INDIAN KISH IN SOUTHERN CALIFORNIA.

wet skirts cling to the ankles and make their wearers uncomfortable."

I have thought a great deal about this, and am not prepared to say that with our present costume I would advocate women's going out much in the rain. But I do say that once in a while they can put on short skirts and stout shoes and such old clothes as cannot be injured by getting wet, and then resolutely and boldly sally forth into the rain, and the harder it comes down the better, if it be warm weather. Then let them learn to enjoy the pattering of the rain upon cheeks and ears. Let them hold out their hands and feel the soft and gentle caresses of the "high-born, noble rain." Let them watch the drops as they spatter on the leaves and trickle down the stems, gathering volume and speed as they reach the bole and fall to the ground, there to give life and nourishment to the whole plant. Everything in Nature loves to be out in the rain. How fresh and bright the trees look after a shower! How the rocks are cleansed and made bright and shining! How their color comes vividly out in the rain! And upon human beings the effect is the same, provided they value health and vigor more than they mind a little discomfort in the bedragglement of their clothes. Years ago I learned this lesson. I was riding from the line of the railway, over the Painted Desert, with several Havasupai Indians. It was the rainy season. Showers fell half a dozen times a day. At first I wished I had an umbrella. I got wet through, and so did the Indians. I thought I ought to feel wretched and miserable, but somehow the Indians were as bright and cheerful as ever, so I plucked up heart and courage, and in half an hour my clothes were dry again. Four or five times that day and an equal number the next day, I got wet through and dry again. Riding horseback kept me warm, and the quick and healthful circulation of the blood, the active deep breathing caused by the exercise, the absence of fear in the soul, all combined to make the wetting a benefit instead of an injury.

My friend W. W. Bass, of the Grand Canyon of Arizona, with whom I have made many trips in that Wonderland region, tells with great gusto a true story of my riding over the desert on one occasion, clothed in one of the old-fashioned linen dusters that reached below my knees. It was warm weather, and dusty on the railway, hence the duster, I suppose. But when we got fairly out on the desert it began to rain, and how it did pour! It came down so rapidly that by and by my pockets were full of water, and Bass says that when he overtook me, I was jogging along, singing at the top of my voice (just as the mocking-bird did), the water splashing out of my pockets as I bounced up and down in the saddle. The linen duster clung to the sides and back of the horse, and wrapped itself around my legs so that the picture was comical in the extreme. But I was happy, and refused to feel any discomfort, and so got joy out of the experience, as well as health and vigor. For let it be remembered that when I came from England, twenty-five years ago, I came as an invalid, broken down in health completely; so much so that I was even forbidden to read a book for a whole year. Now few men are as healthy as I. Years of association with the Indian, learning simplicity and naturalness of him, have aided materially in making the change. I have learned the value of putting the primary things first. I used to be so "nice" and "finnicky" that the idea of having my clothes wet would give me a small panic. "They would get out of shape and look badly, and have to be pressed before I could wear them again." But when I came to the conclusion that I was worth more than clothes, that my health was of more importance than a crease in my trousers, I found I was taking hold of a principle which, while it might at times seem to be rough on my clothing, would have a decidedly beneficial influence on myself.

And this leads to another important lesson we may learn from the Indian. He is not as "nice" sometimes as I wish he were, but we are far too nice, often, for health and comfort. Many a woman ruins her health by wrecking her nerves, drives her husband distracted, worries and annoys her children, by being too nice in her house. I have found, in New England and elsewhere, — aye, even in Old England, — women who valued a clean house more than they valued their own lives, the happiness of their children, and the comfort of their husbands. Indeed, in one case I well remember a woman drove her husband into temporary insanity, and finally into ignominious flight away from her, by her eternal washing of floors, shaking of carpets, polishing of furniture, and dusting down. Every time the poor fellow went in from the workshop he must change his clothes. If he came in from the outside he must take off his shoes before he entered the door. If he put his warm hand down on the polished table he was rebuked, for his wife at once got up, fetched her chamois leather and rubbed off the offending marks. Poor, wretched woman, and equally poor, wretched man! No wonder he went crazy, and finally lost his manhood and ran away.

I know this is an extreme case. But I vouch for its

strict truth. And there are thousands of women (and men too, for that matter) who are afflicted in a serious measure with the same disease. In that home where niceness is valued more than health and comfort and work in life, there lurks serious danger. Go to the Indian, and while I do not suggest that you lose all

HOPI CHILDREN ENJOYING THEIR DAILY SPORT ON THE BACK OF A BURRO.

niceness by any means, seek to learn some of his philosophy and place primary things first. First, health, happiness, comfort, peace, contentment, love; *then* these other things.

I'm going to make a confession that I am afraid will bring me into sad repute with some of my readers.

IN THE RAIN AND THE DIRT

When my first boy was born, we were naturally very proud of him. As he grew out of his baby clothes we liked to see him look nice and neat and clean. He must be a pretty little cherub, dressed in white and have the manners of a Little Lord Fauntleroy. Then I came to the conclusion that we were valuing "niceness" more than the healthy development of the child. I remonstrated and urged a change but to no effect, so I resolved on a *coup d'état*. One morning after the youngster was dressed up in his white bib and tucker, and as uncomfortable and unhappy as any and all healthy children feel at such treatment, I took him by the hand and led him out of doors and out of sight of all watchful eyes, where there was plenty of mud and plenty of water. In half an hour his changed appearance was a marvel. We started a little stream of water, which we then dammed. We made mud pies, and I helped him mix the "dough" in his apron. We reveled in mud from top to toe. I rolled him in it, so that back was as vividly marked as front. Not a remnant of niceness was left in him. We went home happy and contented, laughing and merry, but bedaubed and beplastered everywhere. We had had such a good time. And it was such fun going out with father. We were going again to-morrow and the next day and the next. And so we did. It needed no words, no argument. It did not take long to get two or three suits of brown canvas or blue denim, and the youngster grew up healthy, happy, vigorous, strong, tough, and often dirty, rather than anæmic, miserable, dyspeptic, weak and ailing, and *nice*. There would be far less demand for children's tombstones, surmounted with marble angels and inscribed with wretched doggerel, if mothers valued health rather than niceness, vigor before primness, and strength immaculate rather than bibs and aprons. So I say, let us not be over-nice. And especially let us not train our children to value clean hands and clothes more than the rugged health that comes from contact with the soil in out-of-door employments. I find one can enjoy Homer, and Browning, Dante, and Shakspere, all the better because his body is vigorous and strong, his brain clear, and his mind active as the result of rough-and-tumble mountain climbing, desert tramping or riding, and walking on canyon trails.

Another result of this frank and fearless acceptance of out-of-door conditions is manifested in a readiness to meet difficulties that over-niceness is disinclined to touch. Let me illustrate. Two or three months ago I made a journey with two Yuma Indians and four white men down the overflow of the Colorado River to the Salton Sea. We were warned beforehand that it would be "an awfully hard trip." We were told that it was "hell boiled down" to try to go through certain places. The river for ten or twelve miles left its bed and ran wild over a vast tract of land covered with a mesquite forest. Mesquite is a fairly dense tree growth covered with strong and piercing thorns. When we came to this place we had to cut our way through the thorny thicket, and our faces, hands, and bodies all suffered with fierce scratchings and thorn-pricks. Several times we stuck fast, and there was nothing for it but to jump out into the water with ax in hand and cut away the obstructions or lift over the boat. My Indian, Jim, though dignified and serene, as I shall fully explain elsewhere, had the promptness that over-niceness destroys. He was out over the side of the boat as quickly as I was, ready for the hard and disagreeable work. Had I been "nicely" dressed, and "nice" about the feeling of water up to my middle, too "nice" to wade for hours, sinking into quicksands, in order to find the best passage for the boats, we should have been there yet. We cut down three mesquite trees, under water, in order to get our boats over the stumps. We forced our way through tall and dense arrow weeds, one in front and the other behind the boat, lifting and forcing, pulling and pushing. It was

IN THE MESQUITE FOREST ON OUR WAY TO THE SALTON SEA.

not "nice" work, but it was invigorating, stimulating, and soul-developing.

The other day I went photographing on the Salton Sea. When the launch stopped twenty feet from the island covered with pelicans, where I wished to make photographs, I shouldered my camera, stepped out into the water, which came up to my thighs, and walked ashore. The engineer wondered. Why should he? Had I waited, the pelicans would have flown away. Speed was necessary. "Niceness" would have prevented my getting what I went for. When I stand on the lecture platform, or in the pulpit, or in the drawing-room; when I meet ladies in the parlor and go with them for an automobile ride, I dress as neatly as I can afford, and endeavor to look "nice;" but when I go into my garden to work, I put on blue overalls, a flannel shirt, and a pair of heavy shoes, and I try not to be nice. I roll around in the dirt, I feel it with my hands, I revel in it, for thus, I find, do I gain healthful enjoyment for body, mind, and soul. I owe many things to the Indian, but few things I am more grateful for than that he taught me how to value important things more than "looking neat" and being "nice."

CHAPTER VIII

THE INDIAN AND PHYSICAL LABOR

MINISTERS and orators, teachers and statesmen, members of the W. C. T. U., as well as the Y. M. C. A., of the white race, all profess to believe that the white race believes in the dignity of physical labor.

That profession is often a lie.

We no more believe in the dignity of physical labor than we do in the refinement of a hog. Our actions give the direct lie to our words. I am writing with the utmost calmness, and say these strong words with deliberate intent. As a nation we are humbugs when we pretend to believe in the dignity of labor. Perhaps, after all, we do believe in it, but in most cases it is not for ourselves, but for "the other fellow."

On the other hand, the Indian really and truly believes in the dignity of physical labor. A chief would just as soon be "caught" dressing buckskin, or sewing a pair of moccasins, or irrigating his corn-field as lolling on a Navaho blanket "smoking the pipe of peace." With the white race this is not so. Men believe in the dignity of labor as much as they do in the brotherhood of man. They would no more be seen doing physical labor — wheeling a wheelbarrow, for instance, digging a ditch, building a wall, plowing a potato patch, or doing any other physical work, save the few things men are allowed to do without being thought peculiar, as, for instance, taking care of a small home garden, taking the ashes out of the furnace, and things of that kind — than they would be seen picking their neighbors' pockets or burglarizing their houses. When they want to gain exercise they go to some indoor gymnasium, where the air is the breathed-over, dead air of a hundred people, and they swing dumb-bells, pull on weights, struggle frantically on bars, and do other similar and fool-like things,

A HAVASUPAI GIRL, WEAVER OF BASKETS.

because, forsooth, these things are gentlemanly; or they go out and swing golf-clubs and pursue a poor innocent little ball over the "links," while gaping caddies look on at their wild strokes, and listen to the insane profanity with which they try to compel themselves to believe that they are "gentlemen, bah Jove!"

Of all the contemptible, shuffling, and mean subterfuges the white race is capable of, this seems to me to be about the meanest and most contemptible. To pretend to believe in the dignity of labor, and then at any and all opportunities afforded to labor to dodge away and do these useless and selfish things that do not take off one ounce of the burden of physical labor we have imposed upon our fellows.

Let me not be thought for a moment to be opposed to any healthful recreation or sport. If golf be pursued as a recreation, for fun, I am heartily in accord with it and its promoters. It is when it is taken as an "exercise," as a *substitute for honest and useful labor*, that I protest against it, as a fraud, a delusion, a snare, and a contemptible subterfuge. If you want real exercise, real work, go and relieve some poor fellow-man of his excess of hard work. Tell him you have come to give him an hour's rest, that he may go and study nature, go and look at the flowers of your garden, wander into the woods and hear the birds sing, or visit the public library and read some entertaining and instructive book. If you are too ashamed to openly try to give an hour or two of rest and change to your "brother" man, go and chop the wood for the house, dig up the potato patch, wheel out the manure from the stable, or do some other *useful* and beneficial thing. Pleasure is pleasure, sport is sport, fun is fun, but to engage in these sports seriously, as a physical exercise to counteract the effects of your evil dietetic habits or other grossnesses, is to add hypocrisy and subterfuge to evil living.

What labor the Indian has to do he does gladly, cheerfully, openly. He is not ashamed to have soiled hands or to be caught in the act. In this I am heartily in accord with him. If I ever wrote a creed one of the first articles of my religion would be: "I believe in the benefit and joy of physical labor." If I had my way I would compel every member of the so-called "learned" professions (!), from preacher to lawyer, teacher and doctor, statesman, politician, and bartender, to spend not less than three hours at

HOPI INDIAN WEAVING A DRESS FOR HIS WIFE.

hard physical labor *every day*, and as for my brother preachers, I would put them to road-making every Monday, for half the day at least, so that by practical knowledge of road-making on earth they might be better able to preach to their congregations the following Sunday about the road to heaven. There is nothing that more reveals that we are a people of *caste* and class than the attitude of the rich and the "learned" toward physical labor. I am not in sympathy with that attitude in any respect; I despise, hate, loathe it, and would see it changed. To the Indian, for his honest respect for and indulgence in physical labor, I give my adherence and honor.

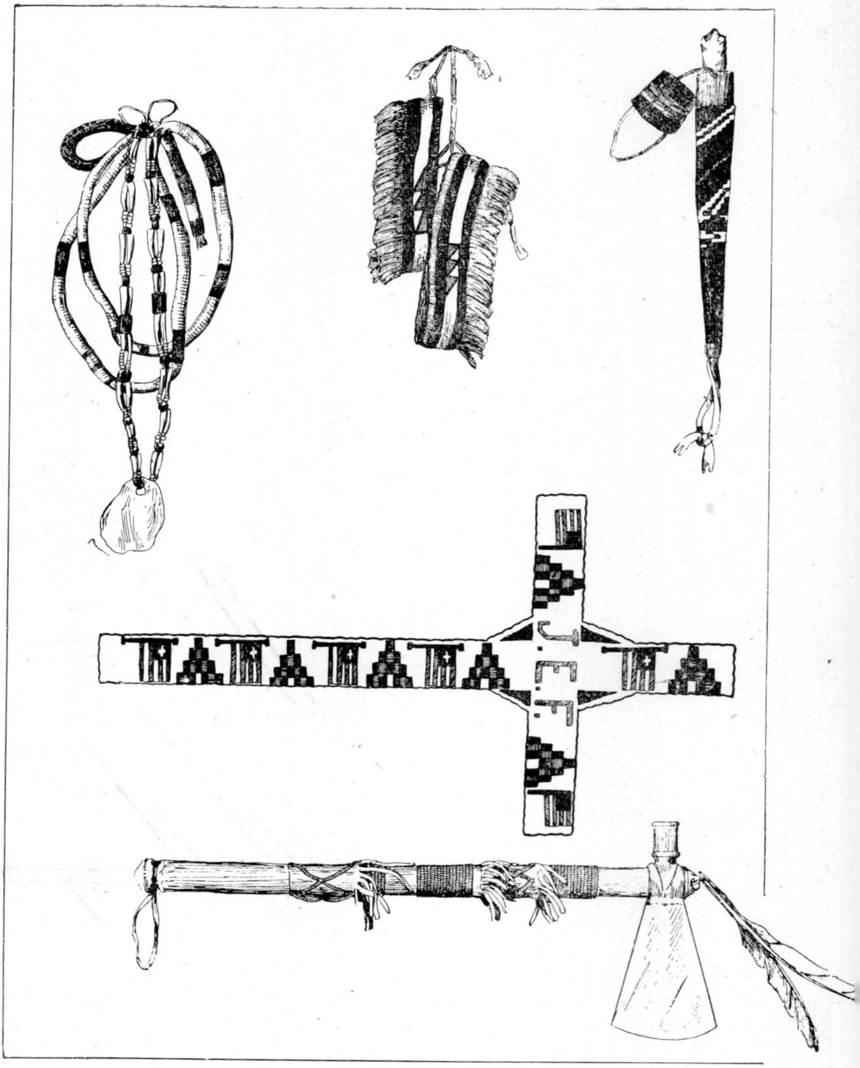

VARIOUS ARTICLES OF USE AND ORNAMENT MADE AND DECORATED BY INDIANS.

CHAPTER IX

THE INDIAN AND PHYSICAL LABOR FOR GIRLS AND WOMEN

IN the preceding chapter I have given the Indian's life, habit, thought, towards physical labor for himself and his sons. He holds the same attitude toward it for his daughter and his wife. And not only does he so hold it, but the wife and daughter regard it in exactly the same way. The out-door life of the Indian girl and woman makes her healthy, vigorous, muscular, and strong. She glories in her physical vigor and strength, and wonders why her white sister is not equal to her in physical capacity. When I tell her that the white women pity her because, forsooth, "she has to do so much hard work, while the lazy men sit by, smoking, and doing nothing," she looks at me in vacant amazement. Once when I was talking in this way one of them said: "Are your white women all fools? Tell them we not only don't need their pity, but we despise them for their habits of life that lead them to pity us. The Creator made us with the capacity and power for work. He knows that all beings must work if they would be healthy. We would be healthy, and therefore we do His will in working at our appointed tasks. We are glad and proud to do them. And as for the men: let them dare to interfere in our work and they will soon see what they will see. We brook no interference or help from them."

So their children (girls as well as boys) are all

brought up from the earliest years to work, and to work hard. Boys are sent out to herd sheep, horses, and cattle; to watch the corn and see that nothing disturbs it. And the girls, as soon as they can toddle, become "little mothers" to their younger brothers and sisters.

HOPI WOMEN BUILDING A HOUSE AT ORAIBI, ARIZONA.

As they grow older they grind all the corn, gather all the wild grass and other seeds, make all the basketry and pottery, and prepare all the food for the household. To grind corn in the Indian fashion, with flat rock and metate, is no easy task for a strong man of the white race, yet I have known a girl of fifteen to keep at work at the metate for ten hours a day for several days in succession, in order that there might be plenty of flour when guests came to the Snake Dance.

On one of my visits to the Hopi village of Oraibi I found the women at work building a house. This is their occupation. All labor among Hopis is divided between the sexes in accordance with long-established custom, and I think it is so divided in all aboriginal peoples. The men undertook the protection of the home (were the warriors) and the hunting of animals for food. They also make the robes and moccasins. Those tribes that lost their nomad character and became sedentary added care of the fields and the stock to the work of their men. The women practically undertook all the rest. The building of the home, its care, the general gathering of seeds, and the preparation of all foods belong to them.

And as a rule, they do their chosen or appointed or hereditary work cheerfully. They know nothing of the aches and pains of their weaker white sisters; they are as strong as men, so they have no fear of physical labor. Not only this, but they enjoy it; they go to it with pleasure, as all healthy bodies do. How often have I stood and watched a healthy, vigorous man swing a hammer at the forge, or in a mine or a trench. How easily it was done, how gladly, how unconscious of effort! To the healthy woman, with reasonable strength, labor is also a pleasure. To feel one's self accomplishing something, and able to do it without undue fatigue or exhaustion, what a delight it is!

The woman who honors us by coming to our house weekly to do the heavy work, often reminds me of a panther. She fairly "leaps" upon her work with an exuberance of strength and spirit that is a perfect delight, in this age of woman's physical disability and disinclination to do physical labor.

So it is with Indian women. They sing in unison

NAVAHO MAIDENS CARRYING WATER OVER THE DESERT.

when a dozen of them get together at the grinding-trough; though the work is hard enough, when long continued, to exhaust any strong man. I have seen women kneel and pound acorns all day, lifting a heavy pestle as high as their heads at every stroke. In the case of these women builders at Oraibi: they carried all the heavy rocks and put them in position, mixed their own mortar, and were their own paddies, and in everything, save the placing of the heavy cross-beams for the roof, to handle which they called upon some of the men for aid, they did all the work from beginning to end.

Now, while I do not especially want to see white

INDIAN MAIDENS TAUGHT BY THEIR MOTHER TO BE BASKET WEAVERS.

women building a house, I do wish, with all my heart, that they had the physical strength to do it or similar arduous labor. I do long for the whole of my race that the women and girls shall have such vigorous health and strength that no ordinary labor could tire them.

"But," say my white friends, — women and girls, — "we don't want to work physically; there is no need

COAHUILA BASKET WEAVER WORKING IN THE OPEN AIR.

for it; we are not strong enough to do it; we exhaust ourselves, and then do not have energy enough for the other duties of life; we engage servants to do our menial labor for us."

Indeed! In the first place I want to protest with all the power I have against the word and idea "menial." There is no menial service. All service, rendered in willing helpfulness and love, is dignified, noble, and ennobling. He or she who accepts service from another with the idea that the service is "menial," thereby degrades himself, herself, far more than the person is "degraded" by the performance of the service. I would rather have my son a good scavenger, working daily to keep the city pure and clean, than be an "honored" lawyer, engaged in dishonest cases; a "successful" politician, tangled up with graft; a "popular" physician, selfishly deceiving his patients; or an "eloquent" and "dear" minister, self-righteously lauding himself and pouring forth inane platitudes in high-sounding phrases from the pulpit. "Menial service" is divine compared with these occupations when they are demoralized.

And the principle of all I have said applies to girls as well as boys. I would rather that daughters of mine should be able to scrub the floor, bake bread, do the family washing and mending, repair the boys' clothes, knit, sew, and take care of the kitchen garden and the flowers, than strum "The Battle of Prague" or "The Maiden's Prayer," without feeling or expression, on a half-tuned piano. The former occupations are holy and dignified as compared with the sham exhibition of the latter. I like to see a girl with an apron on, strong, healthy, willing, useful, capable, engaged in useful household work, and if our young men had one-tenth part of the sense they ought to have, they would hunt for such girls to become their wives and the mothers of their children, rather than for the dainty, white-faced, wasp-waisted, finger-manicured dolls who are useful for no other purpose than to be looked at.

I have no desire to make pack-horses or slaves of intelligent women or girls, but I cannot help asking the question of them: "Which would you rather be, strong enough to do any and all so-called menial and laborious service, and endowed with perfect health, or be weakly and puny and live the life of ease and luxury that most women and girls seem to covet?" And upon the answer to that question should I base my judgment as to the wisdom, intelligence, and fitness for the duties of life of the answerer. There is no dignity in woman superior to the dignity of being able personally (if necessary) to care for all the physical needs of her household; there is no charm greater than the charm of strength combined with gracious, womanly sweetness exercised for the joy of others; there is no refinement greater than the refinement of a gloriously healthy woman radiating physical, mental, spiritual life upon all those who come within the sphere of her influence.

CHAPTER X

THE INDIAN AND DIET

A MAN is largely the result of what he eats. Indeed, many scientific specialists now tell us that sex determination is largely the result of the food eaten by the expectant mother, so that according to what the mother eats the unborn child becomes—male or female. Ploss in his well-known "*Ueber die das Geschlechtsverhältniss der Kinder bedingenden Ursachen,*" Düsing in his painstaking "*Die Regulirung des Geschlechtsverhältnisses bei der Vernehrung der Menschen, Miere und Pflanzen,*" and Westermarck in the "History of Human Marriage," prove conclusively, from close study of actual experimentation, that the sex of the child is largely fixed by the quantity and quality of nutrition absorbed by the mother. Hence it is not too strong a statement that a man is largely the result of his (or his mother's) food.

At first sight it will appear foolish to many of my readers to go to the Indian for ideas on diet, yet I think I can prove, more conclusively than the learned scientists whose books I have named above can prove their theories, that the Indian has many ideas on diet which the white race can learn to its great advantage.

In the first place, the normal aborigine, before he began to use the white man's foods, was perforce compelled to live on a comparatively simple diet. His choice was limited, his cookery simple. Yet he lived in perfect health and strength. With few articles of diet, and these of the simplest character, prepared in the readiest and easiest ways, he attained a vigor, a robustness, that puts to shame the strength and power of civilized men. Why? The reasons are not far to seek. In simplicity of food there is safety. We eat

HAVASUPAI WOMAN MAKING BREAD IN THE OPEN AIR.

not only too much, but too great variety, and every student of dietetics knows that the greater the variety the greater the possibility that too much will be eaten. The Indian, living his simple life, was compelled to be content with the maize, beans, pumpkins, and melons of his fields, the peaches of his orchards, the wild grass seeds, nuts, fruits, and roots he or his squaw could gather, and the products of his traps or the chase. Here, then, was a restricted dietary. He had not much choice, nor a large menu for each meal. The smaller the menu the less, as a rule, any person will eat, be he Indian or white man. The extended menu is a series of temptations to overeat. The simple menu of the Indian was a preventive to gluttony. It will doubtless be recalled that when the great Bismarck was broken down in health, his physicians gave him no other prescription as to food than that he should eat but one kind of food to a meal. This is a dietetic axiom: The less variety the less one eats. In a diseased condition health can often be restored by giving the stomach and assimilative organs less work to do.

Among the Indian race dyspepsia is almost unknown. To this fact that they have a small variety of foods, this healthful condition is largely attributable. On the other hand, one has but to pick up any daily newspaper to see the positive proofs of the dyspeptic condition of the "greatest nation of the world" among the white race. There are nostrums for dyspepsia without end. Syrups, pills, doses that work while you sleep, and dopes that work inside and out. Millions of dollars are annually spent merely in advertising these damnable proofs of our idiocy or gluttony, or both. A thousand nostrums flout their damned and damning lies in the faces of the "superior race"! And a drug store on every corner of our large cities demonstrates the great demand there is for these absolute proofs of our vile dietetic habits. Every pill taken, every nostrum swallowed, is a proof positive of our ignorance, or our gluttony, or our gullibility, and probably a good deal of each. Seventy-five millions of dollars were spent in 1905 in the purchase of patent medicines, every cent of which was worse than wasted.

Before the white race came and perverted — pardon me, civilized — him, what did the "uncivilized Indian" know of patent medicines? What did he know of the diseases which these nostrums are supposed to cure? Nothing! He was as ignorant of one as the other. In his native wildness he was healthy and strong; only since he has been led into evil ways by a false civilization has he so degenerated as to need such compounds.

Let us, then, forget our civilization, — this portion of it, — and forego our physical ills and our patent nostrums, and go back to a simple, natural, restricted diet. In that one course of procedure will be found more restored health than all the physicians of the world can give otherwise in a score of years. Let us learn to eat few things to a meal, and those of such a nature that they will properly mix, and thus not overtax the stomach in its work of digestion.

When I sit down to the laden tables of my rich friends, or at the tables of the first-class hotels of the country, I sometimes find my judgment stronger than my perverted appetite. At such times I look over the bill of fare. I see ten or a dozen courses, varying from cocktails, oysters, and fish to ice-cream, fruit, and wines. There are meats and vegetables, nuts and fruits, cooked and uncooked, pastries and jellies, soups and coffee, wines and spices, sauces, relishes, and seasonings galore, and I am more or less disgusted with the whole business, and eat sparingly of but two or three dishes. At other times, alas! my appetite asserts itself, and I "go the pace" with the rest. Now,

HOPI WOMAN, WITH BODY PARTIALLY EXPOSED, GRINDING CORN AT THE MEAL TROUGH.

when all these things, so elaborately prepared, so daintily served, so "nicely" eaten, are disposed of and in the stomach, let me ask (without any desire to offend): Is there the slightest difference in the contents of the stomach of such a person and the stomach of a hog filled with swill? In the first case there is cocktail and caviar, olives and celery, oysters and soup, fish and entremes, entree and roast, game and punch, ice-cream and cheese, pastry and fruit, nuts and crackers, with water, coffee, tea, or wine to liquefy it all, all taken separately, but now mixed in one horrible mess within, and in the case of the hog they were mixed first and swallowed mixed instead of in "courses."

O men and women of the white race, of the superior civilization, quit such gluttony and disease-breeding courses! Get back to the Indian's simplicity in diet. Learn the meaning of "low living and high thinking." Stop pampering your sensual appetites and feeding your stomachs at the expense of your minds, aye, and at the expense of your souls, for men and women who thus live continuously, generally become selfish, indifferent to the sufferings of others, "proud stomached" — which means much more than it seems to mean — and incapable of the finer feelings.

Nor is this all that the Indian may teach us as to diet. While at times he eats everything he can lay his hands upon and also eats ravenously, in his normal condition he eats slowly and masticates thoroughly. Since Horace Fletcher wrote his most interesting and useful books on diet and life, the term "fletcherizing" has become almost universal amongst thoughtful people to express mastication to the point of liquifaction. But I was familiar with "fletcherizing" before I had ever heard of Mr. Fletcher. The Indians, with their parched corn, had taught me years before the benefit of thorough and complete mastication. I had gone off with a band of Indians on a hard week's ride with no other food than parched corn and a few raisins. This was chewed and chewed and chewed by the hour, a handful of the grain making an excellent meal, and thoroughly nourishing the perfect bodies of these stalwart athletes, who never knew an ache or a pain, and who could withstand fatigue and hardship without a thought.

MY HAVASUPAI HOSTESS PARCHING CORN IN A BASKET.

A marked and wonderful effect of thorough mastication is that it decreases the appetite from 10 to 15 per cent, and reduces the desire for flesh meat from 30 to 50 per cent. The more we masticate the less we desire to eat, and the more normal our appetites become. This in itself is a thing to be desired, for it is far easier not to have an abnormal appetite than it is to control it when it has fastened itself upon us.

Then, too, while Indians will often eat to repletion,

and at their feasts indulge in disgusting gorging, they do know how to fast with calmness and equanimity. I am not prepared to say that they will fast voluntarily — except in the cases of those neophytes who are seeking some unusual powers or gifts from Those Above — yet I do know that several times I have been with them when fasting was obligatory because of the scarcity of food, and they accepted the condition without a murmur. I know a very prominent physician in San Francisco, who has an extensive practice, who pumps the food out of the stomachs of several of his gluttonous patients after their hearty French dinners. He defends his course of procedure by saying that his patients would not listen to him if he counseled fasting for even one meal, yet they are willing to allow him to remove the food after it is eaten, and to swallow some harmless "dope" that he gives them, because that is easy and requires no self-control.

I know the power of appetite; I know how hard it is to eat only that which the reason tells us is best. I know how hard it is to eat slowly and thoroughly masticate the food, but I also know that these things are imperative if one would have perfect health. Therefore, in spite of my many lapses into the old habits, I persist in asserting the good over the evil, and in teaching the good to others, in the hope that, in my own case, the good course will become the easiest to follow, and in the case of the young who listen to me they may learn the best way before they have fallen into the evil way.

There is one other thing the white race might learn from the Indian, and that is that the habitual use of flesh is not essential to health. When Captain

Cook visited the Maoris of New Zealand, he found them a perfectly healthy people, and he states that he never observed a single person who appeared to have any bodily complaint. Nor, among the number that were seen naked, was once perceived the slightest eruption of the skin, nor the least mark which indicated that such eruptions had formerly existed. As Dr. Kress says:

"Another proof of the health of these people was the readiness with which wounds they at any time received healed up. In a man who had been shot with a musket-ball through the fleshy part of the arm, 'his wound seemed well digested, and in so fair a way to be healed,' says the Captain, 'that if I had not known that no application had been made to it, I should have inquired with very interesting curiosity after the vulnerary herbs and surgical art of the country.'

"'An additional evidence of the healthiness of the New Zealanders,' he says, 'is in the great number of old men found among them. Many of them appeared to be very ancient, and yet *none* of them were decrepit. Although they were not equal to the young in muscular strength, they did not come in the least behind them in regard to cheerfulness and vivacity.'"

At the advent of Captain Cook, the Maoris were practically vegetarians; they had no domestic or wild animals on the islands, hence could not have been flesh eaters.

While our Indians of the Southwest will eat some forms of flesh at times, they are, generally speaking, vegetarians. The Navahos scarcely ever eat meat while in their primitive condition, and they are proud, independent, high-spirited, vigorous, healthy, and strong. So with the Havasupais and Wallapais, and most of the aborigines of this region. The Apaches also are largely vegetarians, and yet are known as a fierce and warlike people. They are fierce when aroused, but when friendly are kindly disposed, honest, reliable and good workers, strong, athletic, vigorous, and healthy. These facts demonstrate that flesh meat is not necessary. Meat is another fetich of the civilization of the white race, before which we bow down in ignorant worship. The world would be far better off, in my judgment, and as the result of my observation and experience, if we ate no flesh at all. Personally I am never so well physically and my brain so active as when I live the vegetarian life, though when I am at the tables of meat eaters I eat whatever comes and make the best of it.

The experiences of thousands of healthy and vigorous white men demonstrate that meat is not necessary to the highest development. Weston, the great pedestrian, is both a teetotaler and vegetarian; Bernarr Macfadden and several of his muscular helpers are practical vegetarians; and athletes, business men, lawyers, judges, doctors, clergymen, and many others testify to the beneficial effects of the vegetarian diet. There is no man in the civilized world to-day that works as hard and as continuously, physically as well as mentally, as Dr. J. H. Kellogg of the Battle Creek Sanitarium. He is a rigid vegetarian, and seldom eats more than one meal a day. Yet he works from 16 to 20 hours daily, edits two magazines, writes continually for scientific magazines and periodicals, attends to a vast correspondence, is the business head of the greatest sanitarium in the world, consults annually with thousands of patients, and keeps daily watch of their condition, gives numberless lectures, is always experimenting on foods and surgical appliances and inventing new instruments and methods for curing disease, and at the same time performs more surgical operations, perhaps, with less fatal results, than any other surgeon in the country. Besides this he is the president of the medical college, and lecturer to the students, and gives many lectures to the Medical Missionary Classes, and withal, finds time and strength to confer with, direct the education of, and give personal love to the ten or fifteen children he has adopted into his home and made his own.

Here is an additional item which adds strength to what I have written:

"The attention of medical men has recently been called to the case of Gustav Nordin, a hardy Swede who paddled his own canoe from Stockholm to Paris, reaching there in robust health after the long voyage, during which he lived on apples, milk, water, and bread.

"The *New York Herald* states that this dangerous and arduous voyage was undertaken by the Swede to show what could be done by a man who has given up meat, tea, coffee, wine, beer, spirits, and tobacco. He prides himself in eclipsing those 'vegetarians' who continue the use of tea and condiments.

"When in America, at the age of eighteen, Nordin was suffering so from dyspepsia that he could not take ordinary food. He therefore began a diet of fruit, principally apples, whereby he attained to his present robust condition of health."

So, meat-eating, alcoholic-liquor-drinking white race, cast aside your high-headedness and pride, your dietetic errors and ill-health, at one and the same time, and go and learn of the Indian simplicity of diet, wise limitation of your dietary, careful and thorough mastication, and abstention from all flesh foods.

CHAPTER XI

THE INDIAN AND EDUCATION

TAKE it all in all, I think I believe more in the Indian's system of education than our own,—I mean, in the principles involved. Our education is largely an education of books. We teach from books, we study from books, we get our ideas from books. Joaquin Miller's reply to Elbert Hubbard, before quoted, seems to many people to be a foolish remark. But I see a profound thought in it. It was the poet's protest against the too great use of books. He regards books as subversive of individual thought. He contends that books retard and prevent thought, and that we read, not to stimulate thought, but to deaden it. And undoubtedly too much reading and dependence upon books does deaden and destroy not only thought, but, alas! far worse still, the power to indulge in individual thought. Hence books are often a hindrance and a curse instead of a help and a blessing.

The Indian has no books. While he has tradition and legend, myth and story, he has no written word. Everything that is, as differentiated from everything that is supposed, in his life has to be personally learned by individual contact with the things themselves. Botany is the study of flowers, not of words about flowers. There is but one way we can really study botany, and that is out in the fields with the flower growing before us. It must be seen day in and day out from its planting until its fruition. All its development must be known and understood. The properties of its fruit, its roots, its stem, its leaves, for food, medicinal, manufacturing, or other purposes are all connected with the study. It is well to know the names of the plants, the names of all parts of plants, and the families and species to which they belong, but these latter things, important and interesting though they be, are but secondary or tertiary as compared with the primary out-door personal and intimate knowledge I have referred to.

Those who think the Indian uneducated should read Charles Eastman's (*Ohiyesa*) book telling of his boyhood days with his Sioux parents and grandparents. Eastman is a full-blooded Sioux, and though later educated at Dartmouth College, still shows by his writings and words how much he reveres his wise teachers of the open air and the woods.

The fact is, that in matters pertaining to personal observation the Indian children are far ahead of our own brightest and smartest children; they observe the slightest deviations from the regular order. Who does not know of the Indian's power in trailing. I know Navahos, Mohaves, Hopis, Havasupais, and others who will follow the dimmest trail with unerring certainty, and tell you the details of the actions of the person or animal trailed. This is education of a wonderfully useful kind; a kind that it would be well to give more of to our own children. Indeed, I have been saying, both privately and publicly, for many years, and I here repeat it, that if my children were trained to observe and reflect upon what they observed I should not care if they never went to school until they were grown up to young manhood and womanhood.

That keen, though unusual thinker, Ernest Crosby,

in one of his books, presented the following, which perfectly meets my ideas and suggests what I mean in regard to the Indian:

EDUCATION

Here are two educated men.
The one has a smattering of Latin and Greek;
The other knows the speech and habits of horses and cattle, and gives them their food in due season.
The one is acquainted with the roots of nouns and verbs;
The other can tell you how to plant and dig potatoes and carrots and turnips.
The one drums by the hour on the piano, making it a terror to the neighborhood;
The other is an expert at the reaper and binder, which fills the world with good cheer.
The one knows or has forgotten the higher trigonometry and the differential calculus;
The other can calculate the bushels of rye standing in his field and the number of barrels to buy for the apples on the trees in his orchard.
The one understands the chemical affinities of various poisonous acids and alkalies;
The other can make a savory soup or a delectable pudding.
The one sketches a landscape indifferently;
The other can shingle his roof and build a shed for himself in a workman-like manner.
The one has heard of Plato and Aristotle and Kant and Comte, but knows precious little about them;
The other has never been troubled by such knowledge, but he will learn the first and last word of philosophy, "to love," far quicker, I warrant you, than his college-bred neighbor.
For still it is true that God hath hidden these things from the wise and prudent and revealed them unto babes.
Such are the two educations:
Which is the higher, and which the lower?*

* From Plain Talk in Psalm and Parable, by Ernest Crosby.

I would not have it thought that I am opposed to all systematic and book education, even on our present plan or under our present system. My protest is not

A NAVAHO GRANDMOTHER WITH THE BABY SHE LOVES, AND WHOSE EDUCATION SHE WILL DIRECT.

so wide and sweeping as that. The main propositions upon which I base my opposition are:

1. That we do not pay sufficient attention to the physical health of our students, making health of secondary, tertiary, or quaternary importance, or often not giving it a single thought; leaving it

absolutely to regulate itself, when it should be the first, primary, determinate aim and object of all education.

This very day upon which I write I sat at a professor's table. He is a prominent educator in one of the important cities of the West. We were eating breakfast. He was complaining of indigestion. As he ate I could see his tongue seamed and coated, and his lips were rough and fevered as with stomach trouble. He helped himself to mush, — four times as much as a healthy man ought to have taken, and in far less time than it has taken me to write this he had "shoveled" it all in and "gobbled" it down. (The words in quotation marks are used thoughtfully, and they more truthfully describe what was the absolute fact than any other words with which I am familiar.)

He drank two glasses of milk warm from the cow, and ate French bread which had been heated in the oven and then saturated with butter. The night before he had opened a can of sardines, — as he said, "to see what he could eat," and after the mush he ate a few of them. Then the maid brought in bacon and fried eggs and coffee, and he "did justice" to them. Yet he wondered why he was troubled with indigestion, and his poor wife sent word down from her bedroom that she regretted she could not see me again as she was suffering severely with one of her "regular" sick headaches. My own breakfast consisted of a small quota of mush, some of the hot bread (there was no other), and some cold milk. I felt well and happy after my frugal meal, while he confessed not only to feeling heavy and "logy," but *unsatisfied* with what he had eaten — a clear proof of an abnormal appetite and a disordered digestive system.

Now, is it to be expected that with our teachers themselves so ignorant of the first principles of healthy dietetics our students should know any better? Our

AN AGED COAHUILLA BASKET WEAVER.

whole system of eating is wrong. We eat anything and everything our tastes — often perverted and depraved — demand, and we never ask ourselves the question as to whether the food is good, or our methods of eating it wise and proper. In my chapter on the Indian and diet I discuss this question more thoroughly, but I refer to it in this connection as one of the great defects of our educational system.

2. My second proposition is, that we keep our students indoors all the time, — as a settled, established custom, — with occasional short periods out of doors, instead of reversing the matter and *keeping them out of doors all the time*, with occasional short periods indoors.

Why keep children or university students indoors? While in the winter climate of the East outdoor life is not as possible as it is in the balmy West, there certainly can be much more time spent out of doors than there now is. We pride ourselves upon our scholastic progressiveness, yet they do these things far better in Germany. The educational and medical authorities of Berlin have organized a forest school for the city children of the crowded districts of Berlin and Charlottenburg. In a wide clearing 150 children follow — out of doors — the usual procedure of school, delightfully varied with nature study at first hand. The hours of work are short, and fresh air and exercise are given a supreme importance. The children cook their own dinners at a camp-fire, and their desks and seats and shelter-sheds were made from the timber felled to form the clearing. At 1 o'clock they are all required to take an hour's nap, for which each child is provided with a blanket and a reclining-chair.

This is a move in the right direction. Our schools

cost the nation millions of dollars each year. Surely we have a right to demand that they give us health for our children in exchange, instead of ruining it in so many cases as they now do.

In Japan out-of-door schools are quite common, especially when the cherry and plum trees are in blossom.

In Los Angeles, California, a business college holds many of its class sessions out of doors, and I trust the time will come when this will be the rule in all schools, instead of the exception.

I am perfectly well aware that there is danger that these statements will be taken too literally. They must be taken as broad and general statements. My conception is that in our present condition we *live* indoors and *go out of doors occasionally*. I would have that proposition reversed. We should *live out of doors and go indoors occasionally.*

The same common sense and rational mode of reading my words must be applied to all that I say on out-of-door education. Naturally, I am not such a fool as to suppose that all educational or scientific or any other work can be done out of doors. Though I am not a college professor, and never shall be, though I am not a scientific expert, and never can be, though I am not many things that other men are, I know enough — have observed and seen enough — to know that delicate experiments of a variety of kinds need the most rigid indoor seclusion for their successful conducting. But this does not alter my general propositions, viz., that the health of students is of more importance than any and all education given in schools or colleges; that outdoor life is more conducive to the health of students than indoor life, and that, therefore, *where possible*, all education should be given out of doors.

3. As a result of this indoor scholastic life, we content ourselves by teaching our children from books,—which at best are but embalmed knowledge, canned information, the dry bones of knowledge, words

AN ALEUT BASKET MAKER. THESE WOMEN MAKE THE MOST DELICATE BASKETRY IN THE WORLD.

about things,—instead of bringing them in contact (as far as is possible and practicable) with the things themselves. I believe in books; I believe in education; I believe in schools, in colleges, in universities, in teachers, professors, and doctors of learning; but I do not believe in them as most of the white race seem to do, viz., as good in themselves. They are good only as they are instruments for good to the children committed to their care. The proper education of one child is worth more to the world than all the schools, colleges, and universities that were ever built. One Michael Angelo, one Savonarola, one Francis of Assisi, one Luther, one Agassiz, one Audubon, is worth more to the world than all the schools that ever were or ever will be. And if, by our present imperfect and unhealthful school methods, we kill off, in childhood, one such great soul, we do the human race irreparable injury. Let us relegate the school to its right place, and that is secondary to its primary,—the child. The school exists for the child, not the child for the school. As it now is, we put the plastic material of which our nation is to be formed into the mould of our schools, and regardless of consequences, indifferent to the personal equation in each child, overlooking all individuality and personality, the machine works on, stamping this soul and mind material with one same stamp, moulding it in one same mould, hardening it in the fire to one same pattern, so that it comes forth just as bricks come forth from a furnace, uniform, regular, alike, perhaps pretty to the unseeing eye, but ruined, spoiled, damned, as far as active, personal, individualistic life and work are concerned. The only human bricks that ever amount to anything when our educational mill has turned them out are those made of refractory clay,—the incomplete ones, the broken ones, the twisted ones, those that would not or could not be moulded into the established pattern.

This is why I am so opposed to our present methods. Let us have fewer lessons from books, and more knowledge gained by personal observation; less reading and cramming, and more reflective thinking; fewer pages of books read, and more results and deductions gained from personal experiences with things high and low, animate and inanimate, that catch the eye and mind *out of doors;* and above all the total cessation of all mental labor when the body is not at its best. The crowding of sick and ailing children is more cruel and brutal than Herod's slaughter of the innocents, and so utterly needless and useless that fools couldn't do worse. What is the use of education to a sick person, and especially when the sickness is the result of the educational process. God save us from any more such education!

Doubtless I shall be told that my ideas are impracticable. I know they are and ever will be to those who value "the system" more than the child. Granted that in cold and wet weather students can't get out of doors much. Then open all the doors and all the windows and give up the time to marching, to physical exercises, to deep breathing, to anything,— romping even,— rather than to cramming and studying a set number of pages, while the air breathed is impure, unwholesome, actively poisonous. When our educational methods thus interfere with the health of the child, I am forever and unalterably opposed to them. We had far rather have a nation of healthy and happy children, growing up into healthy and happy manhood and womanhood, even though devoid of much book knowledge, than a bloodless, anæmic, unhappy nation though filled with all the lore of the ages. Give me, for me and mine, every time, physical and mental health and happiness, even though we have never parsed a single sentence, determined the family and

Latin name of a single flower, or found out the solution of one solitary problem of algebra.

4. My fourth proposition is, that as the result of this indoor book-teaching our children are not taught to think for themselves, but are expected and required to accept the ideas of the authors, — often, indeed, they must memorize the exact words of the books. This is, in itself, enough to condemn the whole system. We could better afford to have absolutely no schools, no colleges, no books even, than a nation professedly educated, yet the members of which have not learned to do their own thinking.

5. As a conclusion, therefore, I am forced to recognize that, in a much larger measure than we are ready to admit, our educational system is superficial, is a cramming process instead of a drawing-out — *educere*, educational — process, and no education so-called can be really effective, really helpful, that thus inverts the natural requirements of the mind. And that, when our system ignores the physical health of the student, no matter what his age, it is a criminal, a wicked, a wasteful system that had better speedily be reformed or abolished.

All these ideas are practically the result of my association with the Indian and watching his methods of instruction. His life and that of his family out of doors color all that he and they learn. I think it was John Brisbane Walker who once wrote a story, when he edited and owned the *Cosmopolitan*, about some college men, thoroughly educated in the academic sense, who were shipwrecked at sea. He showed the helplessness and hopelessness of their case because of their inability to take hold and do things. The Indian can turn his hand to anything. When out of doors few things can feaze him. He knows how to build a fire in the rain, where to sleep in a storm, how to track a runaway animal, how to trap fish, flesh, or fowl, where to look for seeds, nuts, berries, or roots, how to hobble a horse when he has no rope, — that is, how to make a rope from cactus thongs, how to picket a horse where there is no tree, bush, fence, bowlder, nor *anything* to which to tie it. What college man knows how to picket a horse to a hole in the ground? Yet I have seen an Indian do it, and have done it myself several times.* He knows how to find water when there is none in sight and the *educated* white man is perishing for want of it, and he knows a thousand and one things that a white man never knows.

As I shall show in the chapter on the Indian and art work, the Indian basket-weaver far surpasses the white woman of college education in invention of art-form, artistic design, variety of stitch or weave, color harmonies, and digital dexterity, or ability to compel the fingers and hands to obey the dictates of the brain.

Education is by no means a matter of book-learning. It is a discipline of the eye, the hand, the muscles, the nerves, the whole body, to obey the dictates of the highest judgment, to the end that the best life, the happiest, the healthiest, and the most useful, may be attained, and if this definition be at all a true one I am fully satisfied that if we injected into our methods of civilized education a solution of three-fifths of Indian methods we should give to our race an immeasurably greater happiness, greater health, and greater usefulness.

*See "Indians of the Painted Desert Region," Little, Brown, & Company, p.15.

CHAPTER XII

THE INDIAN AND HOSPITALITY

ANOTHER of the things I think we might well learn from the Indian is his kind of hospitality. Too often in our so-called civilization hospitality degenerates into a kind of extravagant, wasteful, injurious ostentation. I do not object, on formal occasions, to cere-

THE NAVAHO INDIAN EXPECTS YOU TO PARTAKE OF HIS SIMPLE DESERT HOSPITALITY.

monial hospitality, to an elaborate spread and all that goes with it. But in our every-day homes, when our friends call upon us for a meal or a visit of a week, it is not true hospitality to let them feel that we are over-working ourselves in order to overfeed and entertain them. When one has plenty of servants, the overwork may perhaps not be felt, but the preparation and presentation of "extra fine" meals should be looked upon as an unmitigated evil that ought to cease.

Why is it that the professional lecturers, singers, and public performers generally refuse to accept such hospitalities? Every one doing their kind of work knows the reason. It is because this "high feeding" unfits them for the right discharge of their duties. To

IN THE HOME OF A HOSPITABLE NAVAHO AT TOHATCHI.

overfeed a preacher (and I 've been a preacher for many years) is to prevent the easy flow of his thought. It is as true now as when Wordsworth wrote it, that "plain living and high thinking" go together. For the past five weeks I have been lecturing nightly in New York City. I am often invited to dinners and banquets, but I invariably refuse unless I am promised that a full supply of fruit, nuts, celery, and bread and butter, or foods of that nature are provided for me, and that I am not even asked to eat anything else. I don't even want the mental effort of being compelled to refuse to eat what I know will render my brain "logy," heavy, and dull.

Then, again, when I am invited to a home where no servants are kept (as I often am), and see the hostess worrying and wearying herself to prepare a great variety of "dainties" and "fine foods" for me that I know I am far better without, what kind of creature am I if I can accept such hospitality with equanimity? I go to see people to enjoy them, their kindness, their intellectual converse, the homelikeness of themselves and their children. If I want to "stuff and gorge" I can do so at any first-class restaurant on the expenditure of a certain sum of money. But at the homes of my friends I want them; I go for social intercourse; and to see them working and slaving to give me food that is an injury to me is not, never can be, my idea of hospitality. I would not have my readers infer from this that I am unmindful of the kindly spirit of hospitality behind all of this needless preparation; nor would I have them think that I never eat luxurious things. I am afraid some of my readers would forego their kind thoughts towards me if they were to see me sometimes as I indulge in all kinds of things that "ordinary people" eat. But I do want to protest against the ostentatious and extravagant manifestation of our hospitality, and also the injuriousness of much of it when it comes to the food question, and to commend the spirit and method of the Indian's way. If friends come unexpectedly to an Indian home, they are *expected* to make themselves at home. They are not invited to the "festive board" to eat, but they are *expected* to share in the meal as a matter of course. Hospitality is not a thing of invitation, whim, or caprice.

It is the daily expression of their lives. Every one, friend or stranger, coming to their camp at meal times is for the time being a member of the family. There is no display, no ostentation, no show, no extra preparation. "You are one of us. Come and partake of what there is!" is the spirit they manifest. There is nothing more beautiful to me than to find myself at a Navaho *hogan* in the heart of the Painted Desert, and to realize

HOPI INDIANS COOKING CORN IN AN UNDERGROUND OVEN.

that I am expected to sit down and eat of the frugal meal which the family has prepared for itself.

My contention is, that this is the true spirit of hospitality. You are made to feel at home. You are one of the family. Formality is dispensed with; you are welcomed heartily and sincerely, and made to feel at ease. This is "to be at home"; this is the friendly, the human, the humane thing to do. Unnecessary work is avoided; the visitor is not distressed by seeing his hostess made to do a lot of extra cooking and "fussing" on his account; his heart is warmed by the friendliness displayed (and surely that is far better than merely to have his stomach filled); and, furthermore, if he be a thoughtful man who values health and vigor rather than the gratification of his appetite, he is saved the mortification and the annoyance of having to choose between the risk of offending his hostess by refusing to eat the luxurious "obnoxities"

MOHAVE WOMAN POUNDING MESQUITE TO PROVIDE A DRINK FOR HER GUEST.

she has provided, or offending himself by eating them under protest, and possibly suffering from them afterward.

I was once visiting the Mohave reservation, at Parker, on the Colorado River. It was a very hot day, and I was thirsty, weary, and hot. As soon as I arrived at the home of one old lady, she at once went out of doors to her wooden mortar, took some mesquite beans, pounded them, poured water over the flour thus made, and in a few minutes presented me with a copious drink that was both pleasing to the taste and refreshing. Look at her face as she kneels before the mortar. It is a kindly and generous face. She cared nothing for the fact that it was hot, or that it was hard work to lift the pounder and make the meal for the drink. She did it so simply and easily and naturally that I accepted the drink with the added pleasure that it was the product of a real, and not an artificial, hospitality.

Few visitors to the Snake Dance and the different religious or thanksgiving festivals of the Indians of the Southwest have failed to observe the great amount of preparation that goes on for expected but unknown guests. It is known they will come; therefore preparations must be made for them. Corn is ground in the metates, and *piki* is made.

An old Navaho Indian, pictured on the first page, is a wonderful illustration of the natural generosity of the aborigine before he is spoiled by contact with the white. Many years ago this man, who had large possessions of stock, sheep, horses, and goats, with much grazing land, and several fine springs, was riding on the plateau opposite where the Paria Creek empties into the Colorado River. Suddenly he heard shouts and screams, and rushing down to the water saw a raft filled with men, women, and children, dashing down the river to the rapids. When the raft and its human freight were overturned into the icy waters he did not hesitate because the people were of a different color from his own, but, plunging in, he rescued all those who were unable to save themselves, mainly by his own valor. It turned out that the strangers were a band of Mormons seeking a new home in Arizona, and, being met by the barrier of the Colorado River, had sought to cross it with their worldly goods upon the insecure and unsafe raft.

What could they now do? Though their lives were saved, their provisions were nearly all lost in the raging rapids of the turbulent and angry Colorado. Bidding them be of good cheer, this *savage* Indian led them to one of his *hogans*, where immediately he set his several wives (for the Navahos are polygamists) to grinding corn and making large quantities of mush for the half-famished white strangers. He thus fed them, daily, for months. In the mean time, he allowed them to plant crops (he finding seed) on his land, using for irrigation therefor water from his springs.

But he had not given himself proper care after his icy bath. His legs became drawn up by rheumatism, and from that day to this he has been a constant sufferer from his exposure to the cold water of the river and his after-neglect caused by his eager desire to care for unknown strangers.

The awful irony of the whole thing lies in the fact that in spite of what he had done, the recipients of his pure, simple, beautiful hospitality could not, or did not, appreciate it. He was "only an Indian." He had no rights. *They* were American citizens, — white people; civilized people. Why should this Indian own or control all this fine land, all these flowing springs, all these growing crops? It was wrong, infamous, inappropriate. Therefore, to make matters right, these grateful (?) civilized (! !) Mormons stole from him the best part of his lands, and the largest of his springs, and for years laughed at his protests;

until finally a white friend was raised up for him in a brave United States Army officer, now a general in the Philippines, I believe, who presented the case of the Indian to the courts, fought it successfully, and lived to see the Indian's wrongs in some small measure righted.

To this day the Indian is known as "Old Musha," the name given to him by the people whom he befriended in their distress, because mush was the chief article of the diet that his hospitality provided for them. Truly did Shakspere write:—

> "Blow, blow, thou winter wind,
> Thou art not so unkind
> As man's ingratitude!"

That Indians know how to be beautifully courteous to their guests, I have long experienced. I have eaten at banquets at Delmonico's and the Waldorf-Astoria (New York), the Hotel Cecil (London), the Grand Hotel (Paris), and many and various hotels between the Touraine (Boston) and the Palace of San Francisco and the Hotel del Coronado. And I have seen more vulgarity and ill-breeding at these choice and elaborate banquets, more want of consideration, more selfishness, and more disgusting exhibitions of greediness and gluttony than I have seen in twenty-five years of close association with Indians.

I was once expected to eat at an Indian chief's *hawa*, or house. The chief dish was corn, cut from the cob while in the milk, ground, and then made into a kind of soup or mush. A clean basketful was handed to me, with the intimation that I was to share it with two old Indians, one on my right, one on my left. I asked my hostess for a spoon, for I knew I had seen one somewhere on one of my visits. She hunted for the spoon, in the meantime sending to the creek for an *esuwa* of fresh, clean water. When it was brought, she carefully washed her hands and then gave the spoon seven scrubbings and washings and rinsings before she handed it to me. I felt safer in using it than I do many a time at a city restaurant when the "culled brother" brings me a spoon that he has wiped on the "towel" which performs the multifarious duties of wiping the soiled table, the supposedly clean dishes, the waiter's sweaty hands, and — far oftener than people imagine — the waiter's sweaty face.

During the time we were waiting for the spoon the old Indians by my side sat as patiently and stoically as if they were not hungry. When the spoon was handed to me, I marked a half circle on the mush in front of me, in the basket, then divided the remainder for them. Each waited until I had eaten several mouthfuls before he inserted his own fingers, which served as his spoon, and then we democratically ate together.

Now, to me the whole affair showed a kindly consideration for my feelings that is not always apparent in so-called well-bred strangers of my own race. I 've had many a man light a cigar or a cigarette at a table at which I 've been compelled to sit in a restaurant with never a "By your leave!" or "Is this agreeable?" From the Indian we imagine that we ought not to expect much of what we call "higher courtesy," yet I find it constantly exercised; while from the civilized white race we expect much, and, alas! often are very much disappointed.

It is a singular thing that while I am writing these pages about the lessons we may learn from the Indian, the Bishop of London, speaking in Trinity Church, New York, in September, 1907, should enunciate ideas remarkably similar to those held by the Indians. The Indian owns nothing for himself: it belongs to all his tribe. What is this but the stewardship — in a rude and crude fashion perhaps, but nevertheless stewardship — as declared by the bishop, who says:

"The one sentence, which above all others I would say to you, a sentence as yet unlearned in London and New York, and which if adopted would cleanse the life on both sides of the Atlantic is — life is a stewardship, and not an ownership.

"Have you ever thought why there are any rich and poor at all? That is the question I had to face in London. They had asked me how I reconciled my belief in the good God loving all His children, with the wretched millions in East London, seemingly abandoned by both God and man. I had to face that question, and I have had to face it ever since. There is but one answer — the rich minority have what they have merely in trust for all the others. Stewardship, non-ownership, is God's command to all of us.

"You are not your own. Nothing that you have is your own. We haven't learned the Christian religion if we have not learned the lesson of stewardship.

"My home has been the home of the Bishop of London for 1,300 years. Suppose I should say that it was my own, and that the Bishop's income of $50,000 a year was my own. I would be called a madman. The man who thinks he owns what he has in his keeping is no less a madman. This applies alike to the boy and his pocket money, and the millionaire and his millions. Disregard of this trust is the cause of all the social evils of London and New York."

THE INDIAN AND HOSPITALITY

To resume my experiences with the Indians:

In September, 1907, I again visited the Havasupais and then had several wonderful illustrations of their real and genuine hospitality. We decided to camp below the home of an old friend of mine, Uta. As soon as our cavalcade of six persons on horses, mules, and burros appeared, with two pack-horses, he cordially welcomed us, and when I told him that we wished to camp below his *hawa* he took us into a fenced-in

UTA, MY HOSPITABLE HAVASUPAI FRIEND.

field, where there were peach trees and a corral for our animals. Here we were free from the intrusion of all stray animals, and were able to secure seclusion for the ladies of our party — for, of course, we were camping out and sleeping in the open. Knowing that we should want plenty of water, both for ourselves and our animals, and that it was quite a little walk to Havasu Creek, he took his shovel and in five minutes the limpid stream was flowing through the irrigation ditches close by. The peach tree over our heads —

the best in the whole village — was placed at our disposal, and delicious indeed we found the fruit to be, and he sent us figs, beans, melons, and a canteloupe. Without a question as to payment, he supplied us daily during our stay with an abundance of dried alfalfa hay, — the fresh alfalfa not being good for our too-civilized animals. And in every way possible to him he sought to minister to our comfort and pleasure, and did not resent it in the slightest when I bade him retire at meal times, or while we were cooking our provisions.

MY HOPI HOSTESS WHO KEPT THE NEIGHBORHOOD QUIET WHILE I SLEPT.

That we paid him abundantly when we left did not in the slightest alter the sweet character of his genuine and simple hospitality.

Another illustration of the most beautiful kind of hospitality and courteous kindness was shown by an old Hopi Indian woman pictured. I was visiting the Hopi pueblo of Walpi for the purpose of studying the secret ceremonies of the underground *kivas* of the Antelope and Snake clans prior to the Snake Dance. For fifteen days and nights I never took off my clothes to go to bed, but went from kiva to kiva, witnessing the ceremonials, and when I was too tired to remain awake longer, I would stretch out on the bare, solid rock floor, my camera or my canteen for my pillow, and go to sleep. Occasionally, however, when something of minor importance was going on during the daytime, I would steal upstairs to a room which I had engaged in this woman's house. As soon as I stretched out and tried to sleep, she went around to the children and the neighbors and told them that the "Black Bear"— my name with these people — was trying to sleep, and was very, very tired. That was all that was necessary to send the children far enough away so that the noise of their play could not disturb me, and to quiet any unnecessary noise among their elders. This I take to be an extreme courtesy. I know people of both "low and high degree" in our civilization who resent as an impertinent interference with their "rights" any suggestions that they be kind or quiet to their neighbors, — much less strangers and aliens. But for my own sake I would far rather that my children possessed the kindly sympathy shown by these Indian children than have the finest education the greatest university of our civilization could grant without it.

CHAPTER XIII

THE INDIAN AND CERTAIN SOCIAL TRAITS AND CUSTOMS

IN the treatment of younger children by those who are older, the white race may learn much from the Indian. While it must be confessed that Indian youth are cruel to the lower animals, I have never seen, in twenty-five years, an older child ill-treat a younger one. There seems to be an instinctive "mothering" of the little ones. The houses of the Hopis are built on the edges of frightful precipices, to fall from which would be sure and certain death; yet, although the youngsters are allowed to play around with the greatest freedom, such are the care and constant oversight of the little ones by those who are older that I have never known of an accident.

There seems to be none of that impatient petulance among Indian children that is so common with us; no yelling or loud shouting, and certainly no bullying or cowardly domineering.

Then, too, there is a very sweet and tender relationship existing quite often between the very old and the very young. I know this is not unusual or peculiar to the Indian, but I deem it worthy of note here. I have often seen a grandfather going off to his work for the day in a corn-field with his naked grandson on his back, and the youngster clung to the oldster with an affection and confidence that were absolute.

It should also be observed that respect and reverence are nearly always paid to age. In a council the young

AN APACHE GRANDMOTHER AND HER PET.

men will invariably wait until the old men have spoken, unless they are definitely called upon. If a cigarette is offered to a young man in the presence of his elders, he will not enjoy it until the older ones have lit theirs and taken a few puffs. A girl or young maiden will not sit down until places are found for the older ones and they are comfortably seated, and, of course, the same rule applies to the boys and youths.

It may also seem strange to some of my readers that I insist that the native Indian is inherently honest. I did not use to think so, and I know of many dishonest Indians. But as a rule these are the ones that are partially civilized. They have had so many things given to them without rhyme or reason that they come to regard all things of the white men as theirs. Scores of times I have left my wagon, laden with provisions and other materials, such as cameras, camera plates, clothes, etc., and I have been gone for a week or a month. As I now write I can remember only twice that anything was taken. Once a young man, who had been to our schools, broke into a box of oranges that I had taken as a great luxury after a desert tramp, and ate several of them. I soon learned who the culprit was, made complaint against him, had him brought to my camp, and asked him why he stole my oranges. It must be remembered that it is an unwritten, but well-understood, law of the desert regions that a truly hungry man is always allowed to help himself to needful food, but without waste or extravagance, and with due care for the owner or those who may come after.

This young man claimed that he had taken my oranges because he was hungry. I gave him the lie direct; for, said I, "Had you been hungry, you would have been willing to eat meat and potatoes and bread.

Instead of that you went prowling around until you smelled these oranges and then you stole them. In future, even if you are hungry, you must keep away from my wagon and camp, for if ever you touch my things again, I shall see that you are severely punished." It was a stern reprimand, yet in this case it seemed to be necessary.

The other time that things were taken from me was when I had promised certain women and girls some calico and bead necklaces in return for something they had done for me. Foolishly I showed them the bag in which the calico was. My hostess was also to be a participant in the distribution of favors. While I was away on a several days' exploring trip she took it into her head that she ought to have the first choice, and, as I had promised the piece to her, there would be no harm in taking it. When she had made her own choice, and told of it, of course she could not protest against the others making theirs, so, when I returned to my Indian home I found the bag pretty well looted. It was not long before, little by little, the whole story leaked out. When I was sure, I told my host, and informed him that I wanted every piece of calico and every necklace returned instanter. In twelve hours everything was back in place, as if by magic. Then for several days I kept the promised recipients in a "state," for I intimated that their conduct was so reprehensible that I doubted whether I should give them anything or not. This made them very anxious, and when they "dropped in," two or three at a time, I took the occasion to tell them how I resented their helping themselves to my things while I was absent.

With these two exceptions, in twenty-five years'

experience I have met with nothing but perfect honesty. (No, now I remember, a small whip was taken from my camp many years ago, but when I complained, it was found and returned.) I have left camera plates by the score in boxes that could have been opened, and the results of my months of labor destroyed by nothing but idle curiosity. But when I have explained that I was going away and expected to find everything untouched on my return, I had no fear, no misgivings, and invariably found everything in perfect order when I came back. I doubt whether I could leave things where the whole population of any of our American cities could get at them and find them untouched after a week's or a month's absence.

Another interesting fact about the Indian is that when he gives a name to a child or an adult, it generally means something. Among ourselves names are oftentimes either quite meaningless or senseless. For instance, my parents gave to me the name George. When I was old enough to begin to care about such things, I asked and found out that "George" means "a husbandman." And all through my life I have borne that name — a husbandman — when my ignorance of agricultural pursuits, I am sorry to say, is simply dense and unspeakable. What is the sense of giving such names to children? And when we come to the Algernons, and Reginas, and Sigourneys, and Fitzmaurices, and all the high-sounding but altogether meaningless names with which we burden our children, I long for the simplicity of the Indian's habit, the poetry, the prayer, that so often are connected with the names they give. The old Hebrews knew something of this, for we read of many of their names having a definite and decided significance.

CERTAIN SOCIAL TRAITS AND CUSTOMS

One day I found a Chemehuevi Indian with the name Tow-um-bow-i-si-co-rum. After a little working of it out, I found the name signified: "The reddish golden pathway of glory made by the setting sun from the zenith to the horizon." I asked the man's mother how he came to have such a name, and here is her reply! "As I gave birth to my son, I looked up in the heavens and there I saw the golden reddish glory reaching from above where I lay to the faraway west, where the sun was just setting. So I said, 'It is an omen, and may it also be a prophecy,' and my heart went out in prayer to Those Above, that the pathway of life of my newly-born son might be one of golden glory until he, too, passed out of sight in the west; so I called him Towumbowisicorum, which signifies what I have said."

CHAPTER XIV

THE INDIAN AND SOME LUXURIES

MOST city men regard a shampoo as a city luxury of modern times, except, of course, for the rich, who could always have what they desire. Yet the shampoo is more common with some Indians than with us, and they enjoy it oftener than we do. The Indian's wife takes the root of the *amole*, macerates it, and then beats it up and down in a bowl of water until a most delicious and soft lather results, and then her liege lord stoops over the bowl and she shampoos his long hair and scalp with vigor, neatness, skill, and dispatch. I have been operated upon by the best adepts in London, Paris, and New York, and I truthfully affirm that a white man has much to learn in the way of skillful manipulation, effective rubbing of the scalp, and delicious silkiness of the hair, if he knows no other than such shampooing as I received.

Another so-called luxury of our civilization is an every-day matter with the Indians of the Southwest. That is the Russo-Turkish bath. The first time I enjoyed this luxury with the Indians was on one of my visits to the Havasupai tribe. I had been received into membership in the tribe several years before, but had always felt a delicacy about asking to be invited to participate in this function. But one day I said to the old Medicine Man, as he was going down to *toholwoh*, "How is it you have never invited me to go into *toholwoh* with you?" My question surprised him. He quickly answered, "Why should I invite you to your own? The sweat-bath is as much yours as it is mine." "Then," said I, "I will go with you now."

The "bath-house" consisted of a small willow frame, some six or eight feet in diameter, which, at the time of using, is covered over with Navaho blankets, etc., to make it heat and steam proof. A bed of clean willows was spread out for the "sweaters" to sit upon, and a place left vacant for the red-hot rocks. As soon as all was prepared I was invited to take my seat; one Indian followed on one side and the Medicine Man on the other. Then one of the outer Indians handed in six or eight red-hot rocks, and the flap of the cover was let down and the bath was fairly "on." Directly the shaman began to sing a sacred song which recited the fact that Toholwoh was a gift of the good god, Tochopa, and was for the purpose of purifying the body from all evil.

As soon as the song ended, we were all sweating freely, but when the flap was opened, it was not to let us out, but to receive more hot rocks. As we sang a second song the heat grew more penetrating, so that the words seemed to have real meaning. Our petition was that "the heat of Toholwoh might enter our eyes, our ears, our nostrils, our mouths," etc., each organ being named at the end of the line of petition. The song comprised a great long string of organs, some of which I had never heard of before. By this time sweat was pouring off from our bodies, but the flap was opened only to receive more rocks. At the third time a bowl of water was handed in to my companion, which I was reaching for in order to enjoy a drink, when, to my horror and surprise, he sprinkled the water over the red-hot rocks. The result was an instantaneous cloud of steam, which seemed to set my lips and nostrils on

A MOHAVE INDIAN WRAPPED UP IN HIS RABBIT SKIN BLANKET.

fire and absolutely to choke me and prevent my breathing. Yet the two Indians began another song, so I determined to stick it out and stand it as long as I could. Of course, in a few moments the intense heat of the steam was lost, and then I was able to join in the song. At its close the same process of steaming was repeated, and then I sprang out and dived headlong into the cool (not cold) waters of the flowing Havasu, where for a long time I swam and enjoyed the delicious sensations with which my body was filled. Then, after a rub down with clean, clear, clayey mud, and another plunge, I lay in the sun on a bed of willows, listening to the Indians tell stories, and I can truthfully say I never felt so clean in my life.

This bath is taken by thousands of the Southwest Indians once a week as a matter of religion, so that, as a fact, while their clothes are ragged and dirty, and they themselves appear to be dirty, they are really clean. It must be confessed, on the other hand, that too many Americans value the appearance of cleanliness more than the reality. They would far rather appear clean even if they were not than *be* clean and appear dirty. It is better to combine both reality and appearance, but, for my own sake, if I had to choose between the two, I believe I would rather *be* clean than only *appear* clean.

Civilized man, for centuries, has used hot baths of various kinds for remedial and healing purposes. Throughout the world, wherever hot springs are found, men and women congregate in large numbers, palatial hotels are built, bath-houses established, and an army of hotel-keepers, physicians, nurses, masseurs, and bath operators organized. Some go to the baths just as they do any other fashionable thing, or in order to mingle with the gay and fashionable throng. Other idlers go purely for the pleasure they gain from such associations, while still others go for the health they long for, — the strength and vigor they have lost. And there can be no question that they often gain it. In spite of the fashionable doctors who care less for the health of their patients than they do for their own fame and pockets; in spite of the physical ills that come from the altogether inappropriate diet of the hotel dining-rooms; in spite of the excitement of balls and parties, receptions and routs, common at such places; and in spite of the injurious influences of the gaming tables too often maintained, the use of the waters is often beneficial to a number of the patients. Were they to use the waters rationally, live hygienically, avoid all stimulating foods and drinks, and religiously refrain from all unnatural excitements, there is no question but that the use of the hot waters, the hot mud packs, and the like, would give health to many thousands who now derive but little benefit from them.

From whom did the white race learn the use of the hot bath, the mud bath, and the like? He learned it from the Indian, and if he would study the present methods of the Indians he would find many details connected with these baths that he might learn to his great advantage.

When the Indian goes to the bath he makes of it an almost religious ceremony. In one of the illustrations an old Indian Shaman is telling to the younger ones the things they should heed before going into the *toholwoh*, or sweat bath, the frame of which (as yet uncovered) is close at hand. The hot waters that bubble out from the interior of the earth he regards as the special gifts of the gods. He prays that he may not use these gifts unworthily. Just as the Mohammedan believes that the desert is the "Garden of Allah" and that no one must walk in it who is sinful until he has first asked for forgiveness, so does the Indian believe that the waters of healing will turn to his injury if he does not use them in the right spirit. Would it not be well if we — the superior race — approached this good gift of God in like manner?

The natural simplicity of the Indian at the baths also offers a good lesson to us. Instead of seeking for gaiety,

THE SHAMAN TELLING THE STORY OF THE FIRST TOHOLWOH.

frivolity, fashion, and the means of pampering his appetite, he goes to the baths of nature resolved upon quiet and restfulness as far as possible. He seeks to prepare his mind beforehand, that the physical means used will be beneficial. In other words, though he is a rude, untutored savage, — so we say, — he has a clearer conception of the effect the mind has upon the body in real, practical healing, than has a large part of his civilized brothers and sisters. As a rule, we go to a physician, or to a sanitarium, or to baths — I mean those of us who are sick and desire health first of all — without any other thoughts than "I am sick.

To go here may do me good. I hope it will." Instead of preparing our minds beforehand by thoughtfulness, getting ourselves into the proper mental attitude to be helped, we leave it to chance, to the surroundings, to the doctor, and thus often fail to get the benefit we might have received. We carry our business cares, our family worries, our money-getting, with us and thus defeat the end for which we go.

Nor is that all! When we get there we want "all the comforts of a home." In other words, we must be assured that we have a bedroom which we can lock up at night, a bedstead with a mattress as soft and unhealthy as the one we regularly sleep on, stuffy closets where we can hang our clothes,—and the rest.

The Indian finds his bedroom under the stars. He puts the invalid flat on the ground,—a sheepskin, perhaps, between him and the earth, but that is all. When will the superior white race learn that rejuvenation of the body comes quicker to those who "shed" their civilization, forswear their home comforts, quit their indulgence in fixed-up dishes, refrain from social frivolities (commonly called duties), and first and foremost,—after throwing away all the cares and worries that come of being so highly civilized,—get to a place where it is possible to sleep out of doors *on the hard ground*, protected, of course, as the Indians are. Get into the woods, on to the hills, down in the canyons, out on the deserts. Take a roll of blankets along, and no matter what the weather, learn to sleep on the bosom of Mother Earth, out of doors. And if the region is one near hot springs or mud baths, all the better. Make it for the time being your home.

Ah! how wise is the Indian in his choice of a home. I have before referred to this, but I cannot help writing of it again. Home! It is not a place of unrest to him, where it requires the labor of wife and daughter, or a host of servants, to keep it in order; where polished furniture, polished floors, polished doors, polished mirrors, keep one forever with wiping-cloth in hand, removing the marks of careless fingers; where bric-a-brac is accumulated and piled everywhere to the shattering of nerves if the children get near it, or careless visitors happen to call; where "social demands" are so great that children are relegated to the care of servants; where brothers and sisters scarce have time to know each other, and husbands and wives meet semi-occasionally — no, it is not a home of this kind. To most Indians "everywhere" is home provided there is a little shade, water, and grass for his burro or pony. In the mountains, where he can shelter under an overhanging rock, or in the forest where he has a roof of emerald, supported by great pillars of pine or cottonwood or sycamore, — there is home. In the desert, where the roof is millions of miles high, decorated with suns and moons and stars and comets and meteors and Milky Way and countless nebulæ, and the walls are bounded on the east by the rising sun, and on the west by the setting sun, and God's own laboratories make new, fresh, pure air every moment — there is home.

The San Francisco disaster taught thousands of people the healthfulness of the outdoor life. People who had been ailing for years, puny children, anæmic youths and maidens, dyspeptic parents, all "picked up" appetite and health when compelled to live in the parks and on the streets.

Let us heed the lesson. Let us follow the example of the Indian and be more simple, more natural. Let us relegate to the museum the collecting of curios and bric-a-brac and the thousand and one things that so crowd our houses as to make museums rather than homes of them.

I do not suppose it is necessary that I should say that in our civilization we cannot *literally* do as the Indian does in this matter. That is not my thought. What I would urge is that we live more simply, and that, like the Indian, we get out of doors more, instead of housing ourselves the more as we become more "civilized." And that, in the arrangements and accumulations of our home we make personal health, comfort and happiness the most important considerations, rather than display, and to win the approval or envy of our neighbors.

A MOHAVE WOMAN WHOSE HAIR HAS BEEN "DRESSED" IN MUD.

But to return to the hot springs. The Indian has always used them. He also learned and bequeathed to us the knowledge that mud is a useful therapeutic agent. The Yumas, Mohaves, and others who live near the banks of the Colorado River are in the habit of regularly plastering down their hair and scalp with thick, black mud. They go where it is clean and fresh, — washed down by the rushing waters of the mighty

Colorado through the great canyons — and, rubbing it well into their hair, they cover it over with a cloth tied over the scalp and go on about their daily work. They keep the hair thus covered with mud for a day or two, and then wash it off and give the scalp a thorough cleansing. What is the result? Whether the fact be a result from the use of the mud or not, it *is* a fact that these river Indians have long, glossy black hair free from all disease, and their scalps are as healthy as the hair. They have no dandruff, no falling out of the hair, and do not need any hair tonic or dye. The mud contains enough of the finely ground sand commingled with the softer silt to make a healthful mixture for gently exciting the scalp when the rubbing off and cleansing process takes place. And covering the hair as well as the scalp with the mud and allowing it to dry on demands that the hair shall be well rubbed as well as the skin. The effect is to clean the hair thoroughly, and who knows but that the excitement generated by thus rubbing the hair as well as the scalp has something to do in promoting the healthful flow of the elements required for hair nutrition? Be that as it may, I know the fact, which is that these Indians, men as well as women, have hair, long, black, glossy, reaching down to their waists, and they attribute its healthfulness to the regular use of the mud-pack and rub.

Now, while we may not care to pack the hair in mud, we can certainly utilize the idea. I have done so for years. I often give my scalp and hair a mud bath, and it is both agreeable and exhilarating, and I had the assurance a few months ago from one of the leading scalp specialists of the East that my scalp was in an absolutely healthful condition — one of the very few found in such condition in the large eastern metropolis.

The Indian also uses mud — and by this I mean the clear, pure, uncontaminated earth and sandy mixtures found in the rivers of the desert west — for wounds. There is little doubt but that he learned this from the animals. Who has not seen a dog, after a fight in which he got worsted, run and throw himself into a

A MOHAVE INDIAN WHOSE HAIR AND SCALP HAVE BEEN CLEANED WITH MUD.

mud puddle? Many years ago — about twenty — I read an account of a battle between a wildcat and a dog, and the writer, who saw the conflict, told how the dog went and bathed himself in mud thereafter. The brief sketch made such an impression on me that I knew just where to find it, and I have hunted it up, and am now going to copy it for the benefit of my readers. It will help explain why the Indian does the same thing. He has observed the animals bathing in the mud, when wounded, as this dog did.

"The dog has won the battle; but he has got some ugly scars along his sides and flank. Observe, that overheated as he is, he does not rush into that clear stream. He takes his bath in that shallow spring with a soft mud bottom. Note how he plasters himself, laying the wounded side underneath, and then sitting down on his haunches, buries all the wounded parts in the ooze. That mud has medicinal properties. The dog knows it. No physician could make so good a poultice for the wounds of a cat's claws as this dog has found for himself. Pray, if you had been clawed in that way by either feline or feminine, would you have found anything at the bottom of your book philosophy so remedial as this dog has found?"

The Indian's use of mud, therefore, is seen to be an inheritance as the result of his observation of the animals. Since the time I heard of the dog and wildcat fight I have had occasion to watch the Indians many times. I have used the mud with them, and always with good results. And if, when some four and a half years ago I was bitten on the thumb by a rattlesnake, and for a week was supposed to be hovering between life and death, I had thought enough to have done as the Indians do, — gone and put my hand and arm in a mud bath at the side of a stream or at the bottom of a shallow spring, I should have fared as well as I did (and perhaps better), though I had two skilled physicians, an accomplished professor, and a devoted nurse to care for me.

And when I was supposed to be well again, — months afterward, — I found that the deadly poison had in some way lodged in the lining of the stomach, so that, at times, it would cause a nervous and muscular disturbance that made me suffer intense agony. I then recalled the use of mud by my Indian friends, and I hied me away as speedily as I could to the hot mud baths of Paso Robles, in California. There the sulphur water at a temperature of over 110° Fahrenheit comes bubbling into a great wooden tank filled with the soft, velvety mud, black as ink, of the tule marsh. Into this tank I stepped, and gradually worked my way into the mud, lying down in it, and wriggling and working my body until I was as near covered as I could be. I brought great armfuls of the hot, soft, and soothing nature poultice over my stomach and body, and then lay there as long as it was wise to do so. What mattered it that I was blacker than a negro when I came out. Two minutes with a bucket and a hose and I was cleaner than ever. One week of these baths and I lost the poison, never again to return. I never think of Paso Robles and the mud baths there without a deep sense of gratitude that some of us at least have learned how to utilize some good things that the Indian has taught us.

CHAPTER XV

THE INDIAN AND THE SEX QUESTION

HAVING studied medicine somewhat in my life, I have been permitted as a "medicine man" to know more of the intimate life of the Indian women than many white men. In this article I propose to give the results of many observations in this field, with full assurance that there are many things the white woman may learn from the Indian, both in her treatment of herself and her children.

In the first place, the period of adolescence in both boys and girls is regarded with the importance it deserves.

The white race has much to learn from the Indian in its treatment of boys and girls at this age. My blood is made to boil almost every day when I am in our cities and see young girls, just entering into maidenhood, coming home from school, anæmic, pale, nervous, irritable, almost victims of St. Vitus's dance, often dyspeptic or with a cough fastening its hold upon them, because their parents are so blind and foolish as to prefer book and school education to health. To me such parents are guilty of cruelty and criminality, and I would sooner imprison them and take away the control of their children from them than I would the forger or the housebreaker. They are cruel in that they are either ignorantly or wilfully ruining the health, — perhaps for life, — of their children, and they are criminal in that by so doing they are injuring the future welfare of the state. Boys, too, are treated exactly the same at this time as at any other, and when the great mystery of sex awakening is upon them, they are sent to school as usual, treated with the same untrue answers to the questions that arise that they were given to quiet their minds when they were little more than babies. I am thankful there has been much of an awakening in this matter during the past twenty years, and that I have had an active part in it. I think it was in 1888 that I published a small book on sex teaching for the young.* It is as imperative to warn the young to-day as it was then. The Indian boy is instructed fully into the mystery of sex just as soon and as simply as he is in every other question that arises, and at puberty he is made the subject of specific ceremonies that teach him the meaning of the change that is coming over him. He is treated with a new dignity, is formally recognized as having entered man's estate, and is sent out into the woods or the solitude of the desert "to come to himself."

In the case of girls, ceremonies of instruction, purification, and dedication are almost universally observed. The adolescent is set apart from her fellows, and the elder women give her definite and full instruction as to what the change that is taking place in her life means. She is shown the importance of the new function, and how much the welfare of the race depends upon it. Then she is made to undergo ceremonies that last for several days, in which her body and all its functions are dedicated to the tribe. She is one of the future mothers now, and, as such, is entitled to all respect and consideration. There is no foolish reserve, no "mod-

* "The Guiding Light," in two parts, to be had only from the author, 1098 N. Raymond Ave., Pasadena, Cal. In paper, 50 cents; in cloth, $1.00 postpaid.

esty," so-called, which arrogates to itself the right to criticise the wisdom of God in creating human beings male and female that they may marry and propagate their kind upon the earth. For, wherever one finds the sort of "modesty" that is ashamed of natural and God-given functions, there is either a mental perversion for which the victim is to be pitied, or a moral perversion which is to be reprobated. Every Indian girl is given fully to understand what the function means, with all its possibilities, and she is taught to pray that, when the time comes, she may have a lover, and that he may be a good husband, and that, in due time, she may be the happy and healthy mother of many happy and healthy children.

And in some tribes there are certain shrines where the girls are taught to go and offer their prayers that lovers, husbands, and children — not one or two of the latter, but many — may be given to them at the will of the gods above.

This is to dignify sex, to train the girls that wifehood and motherhood are holy and to be desired, and that they are not matters merely to jest and joke about, or to talk in secret whispers about one to another, as if the very subject were unholy and unclean.

Then a matter of practical healthfulness is observed that white parents need very much to learn, it appears to me, especially in this age of scholastic crowding and mental overworking. Each month the girl is required to rest, in order that she may preserve and maintain her body in perfectly healthy condition. She may go where she will, but she must be quiet and still, in order that the function may be not disturbed, and that its regularity may be established. Not only this, but this habit of rest is kept up so long as the function continues through life. Even on the march a woman may stay behind (if she so desires) and rest for a day or so. The result of this rest at such times is shown in the strength and vigor the women show during pregnancy and at birth. They seem to store up strength, and, as I shall later show, childbirth to most of them is no more a time of peril, pain, or distress than is breathing.

A HAVASUPAI MOTHER, PROUD OF HER MAN-CHILD.

Mothers who neglect to thus instruct and care for their daughters at the adolescent period are criminals both to their children and to the race. Among the ancient Greeks such a mother would have been regarded as a monstrosity; yet many mothers have confessed to their physicians they have never had one word of converse with their daughters upon this most important subject. When I see children going to school at this adolescent period, and being forced by our competitive system of education to strain every nerve to cram the required amount of facts into their brains, I do not wonder that we have so many sickly women who are incapable of being the mothers of healthy and happy children. Far better that our children be not educated in chemistry, and literature, in physical science and art, than that they unfit themselves for the happy relations of a beautiful marriage and sweet and tender parenthood. For let the new or the old woman say what she will, the divinely ordered plan is that women shall be wives, and happy wives at that, capable of making their husbands happy, or at least of contributing their share to that end, and also that they shall know the joys of maternity. Unhappy indeed is that woman whose physical condition is such that she refuses to know the sweet touch of her own baby's body, and denies herself the blessed privilege of training its soul for a beautiful and useful life.

The Indian mother sees to it that her daughter is early taught her future possibilities and the will of Those Above in regard to her, and the growing woman would as soon shirk the responsibilities of her sex as she would refuse to eat. The consequences are that normal births with Indian women are practically painless and entirely free from danger. I have known a woman to deliver herself of her child, sever the umbilicus, and then walk half a mile to the creek, walk into it with the baby, and give herself and the child a good washing, then return to her camp, suckle the little one, and proceed to attend to her duties as if nothing had happened. At another time I saw a woman, less than half an hour after her child was born, start off for a heavy load of wood. Their freedom from constricting waist-bands, their absolute freedom of body, their nasal and deep breathing, their muscular exercise through life, their open air sleeping and living, — all have much to do with these easy births.

To a good Indian woman, also, there is nothing more evil than to circumvent the will of Those Above by refusing to have children. Such a woman would be almost a monstrosity to an Indian, who would be unable to comprehend the mental workings of such an abnormality. Children are to be desired, to be longed for, and to become a joyous possession. In the making of some of their basketry the Paiuti women weave a

THE AUTHOR DESCRIBING THE SYMBOLISM OF THE PAIUTI BASKET DESIGN.

design which shows the opening between the upper and lower worlds through which the souls of all children born into this upper world must come. By a correspondence of the symbol with the thing symbolized, the

Paiuti weaver believes that if she closes up this opening in the basket, she will render herself incapable of bearing any more children. Therefore, even though you were to offer her her weight in money, you could not persuade her to close up the aperture in the basket's design. This would be circumventing the will of the gods.

The same law, too, applies to the suckling of her child. The Indian mother never dreams of foregoing this healthful duty and pleasure. She regards it as one of her special joys, in which she is superior to man. And just as the Paiuti weaver refuses to close the aperture in her basket, so does the Zuni woman refuse to close, except with averted eyes and a prayer that the gods will see she did it with unseeing eyes, the tiny aperture in the mammæ of the water bottles which she makes of clay in imitation of the human breasts. She dare not, even thus in symbol, suggest the closing of her own maternal founts.

Ah! beautiful simplicity and joy of naturalness. The God of men and women surely knew what was good for them when He set in motion the forces that created them. In harmony with His will and purpose we are healthy, happy, normal beings, living lives of purity, progress, and peace. In opposition to His will we are unhealthy, unhappy, abnormal beings, full of wretchedness, impurity, and misery. In many things the Indian, too simple to go far away from the Divine precepts which come to him through contact with nature, is wiser than we. Let us then put on the garment of simplicity, seek to know the will of God, and with hearts like little children learn the true way, and then seek for courage to walk therein.

A HEALTHY AND HAPPY PIMA MOTHER WHOSE BABY WAS GLADLY WELCOMED.

CHAPTER XVI

THE INDIAN AND HER BABY

I HAVE elsewhere spoken of the Indian woman's reception of her child. It is welcomed with joy, and yet in its first hour's treatment most white women would think its life would terminate. After seeing that it breathes properly — that is, through the nose — the mother carries her little one to the nearest creek or water-hole and gives it a good bath. Cold water has no terrors for her, and she does not fear its use for the child. With this cold bath the child may be said to enter its earthly existence. Henceforth life is to be a succession of hardening processes. Indian babies get no foolish and weakening coddling. They are loved dearly and petted often, but are made to lie down on flat boards or basket cradles, with arms and legs strapped down, and are thus early accustomed to physical restraint. They sleep out of doors from the day of their birth, and become accustomed to all kinds of weather. For an Indian child who has taken cold we shall look in vain. The name, the thought of such an ill is unknown.

If the parents have to move from canyon up to plateau, or go off to far away forests for the winter's supply of pinion nuts, the child is put into its carrying basket, swung on the back of the mother, dependent from her forehead, and carried either on horseback or on foot to the new stopping place. Simplicity and naturalness accompany every stage of the little one's life until the age of puberty, when the child-life is supposed to end, and the man or woman life begins.

Now, while of very necessity our method of treating white children must be different from this, we can learn many lessons from the Indian that will materially benefit our race. The key-stone of the whole idea is found in the words: "No coddling." Not long ago I went to the home of an artist friend. His wife had just presented him with a fine, healthy son. The wife's mother was present, and had taken charge of the young mother and her baby. The room was stifling hot, so that I could scarcely breathe, and when I went to see the baby it was wrapped up in a cradle with a sheet and *three* blankets *over its head.* At once I opened the doors and windows, taking good precaution to see that the mother did not take cold. I gave both grandmother and new mother a lecture upon the monstrous folly and cruelty of thus depriving the new-born child of needed air for its expanding lungs. The lesson was accepted in the proper spirit, for the father fully agreed with me, and on the grandmother's departure, a few days later, the coddling, smothering process ceased, and a cold bath, sleeping out of doors, and a generally healthy treatment of the child substituted. I know this is an exaggerated case, but it serves as an illustration of the wrongful and excessive

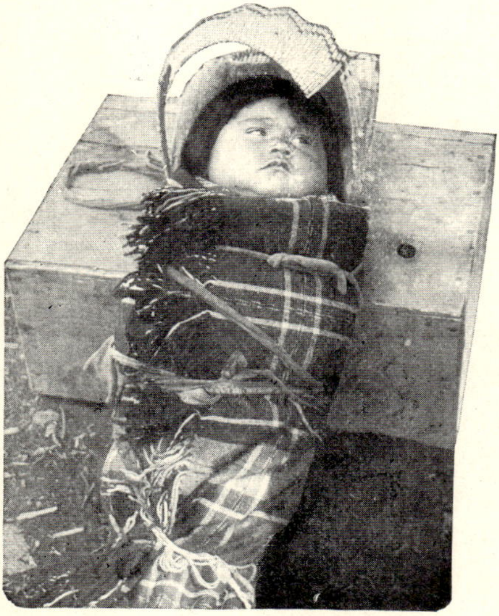

A HEALTHY AND HAPPY INDIAN BABY.

"coddling" we give our children, from which follow such evils as weak lungs, weak throats, readiness to take cold, etc.

As the exaggerated opposite of this, let me relate the treatment I accorded to my own children.

When my first son was born, we were so located that I was compelled to be both physician and nurse. His first experience — after a good hot bath — was a cold bath, and within half an hour of his birth he was sleeping out of doors. At five weeks of age he and his mother accompanied me on an eight-hundred-mile drive over the plains and deserts of Nevada. We camped out, slept on the ground, and gave him, whenever possible, an open air bath in the cold mountain brooks that occasionally were met with.

A year or so after the second boy was born I was stationed in the little town of Cedarville, Cal., and one of the happiest remembrances of my life there was in winter when the snow was deep upon the ground. I would place a canvas upon the floor of my small study, where a good fire blazed in the stove, fetch in a couple of washtubs full of snow, then undress the youngsters, and watch them as they sat in the snow, rubbed it on their naked bodies and laughed and shouted and crowed with delight when I gently snowballed them.

While they were little tots, every morning before being dressed they stood outside while I threw — not poured, but threw, — a bucketful of cold water over them. Then, after a vigorous and hearty rub down, they went with me for a walk where they were allowed to run and jump and romp to their heart's content.

This I call a rational treatment of children. It certainly is a healthy treatment, and those brought up under such an Indian method will never know the aches, pains, ills, and weaknesses that most white children are afflicted with. And I would treat my baby girls, if I had any, exactly the same as my boys, for the health of the race more nearly depends upon the health of the future mothers than upon that of the future fathers.

If it be thought that I am too extreme I quote an article entire from a recent *Good Health*, entitled "Strenuous Health Culture," in which it will be seen that others have done the same thing with equally good results.

> "'Time was when clothing, sumptuous or for use,
> Save their own painted skins, our sires had none.'

"Yet they were far healthier and hardier than the present much-clad generation. Why does the savage go naked with impunity while the civilized man shivers in his clothes, and is a prey to colds, pneumonia, and a variety of diseases unknown to the naked savage?

"One of the marvels of the normal human body is its wonderful adaptability — the maintenance of its equilibrium under constantly varying conditions. By the regulation and adaptation of the heat functions of the body the bodily temperature is maintained at the normal standard in spite of the changing temperature of the surrounding atmosphere. But when the body is artificially heated continually, as by over-clothing and over-heated rooms, its functions become to some degree dormant, and in consequence the natural bodily resistance is greatly lessened.

"The effort of the body to resist cold stimulates and strengthens. One who can resist cold can resist all kinds of disease germs. This has been demonstrated by the success of the 'cold-air cure' for a variety of diseases.

"The old-time coddling of delicate children, which still further lessened their vitality and weakened their powers of endurance, is now giving place to its opposite. Judicious exposure to cold has been found to be one of the best methods of strengthening weak infants and developing healthy children. At a recent conference of mothers held in Minnesota, they were advised that a snowbank makes one of the best cradles. One mother who had tried this treatment thought that it accounted for the unusual health and strength of the family.

"A Milwaukee physician, Dr. John E. Worden, has adopted this strenuous treatment to prepare his babes for the rigors of life, and up to the present his methods have been abundantly justified by their success. His little daughters, Shirley and Jane, aged respectively eight and three years, are two of the firmest and healthiest bits of humanity to whom disease of all kinds is unknown. During the cold weather these children may be seen barefooted and bareheaded, clad only in their cotton garments, thoroughly enjoying a romp in the snowdrifts, and without even a goose-pimple on their skin.

"'We are merely following out health rules,' said Dr. Worden, speaking of his unique methods of bringing up his children. 'We are aiming at prevention rather than at cure. We have brought the children up so that they are fearless, and dread neither the ice-cold plunge nor a romp in the snow in their bare feet. The door is always open, and they go out when they like and return when they are ready to do so. We do not force the children to go out in the snow barefooted;

A HOPI INDIAN AT ORAIBI SHELLING CORN.

they go out of their own free will, and play until they are tired, or their attention is called to something else.

"'In the summer we send them out into the sun bareheaded and barefooted, with orders to keep out of the shade. On the street cars they are instructed to sit on the sunny side of the car. It is well that they experience something of contrast; therefore, a cold bath is given them daily in the warm weather. In the winter they are allowed to go outdoors to get stimulus from the cold air.

"'Children brought up like tender hot-house plants are likely to contract colds and other diseases, and to die as the result of not having robust constitutions. These children, on the contrary, will and do escape without any sickness; and should they get sick, their recovery is almost certain, because of their being strong and in good condition.'

"Both Dr. Worden and his wife are graduates of the University of Michigan, and Mrs. Worden was for a number of years before her marriage a trained nurse.

"'During my hospital training and institutional work,' says Mrs. Worden, 'I saw so much sickness due to weakened bodies that I investigated causes, and came to the conclusion that much of the weakness was due to a lack of physical development, to abuses through mistaken kindness on the part of the parents, that so weakened the immature bodies that they could not withstand the attack of disease. With our children, beginning from babyhood, we have had one aim, and that is to give them strong physiques, and we have succeeded thus far. They have never had one drop of medicine, and never been ill one moment.'

"The clothing of these children is always light, and much the same summer and winter. It is of cotton almost exclusively, and no bands are ever used. In the place of stockings the easy, sensible, comfortable Roman sandal, made only in England, is worn.

"'We believe in clothing them as lightly as possible,' says Mrs. Worden, 'depending on their excellent heat-making organs to develop any extra warmth needed in an emergency. This stimulates a necessity for a good, strong internal circulation of the fluids of the body, and creates a desire to exercise a little in order to keep warm. Over-warm children are usually lazy.'

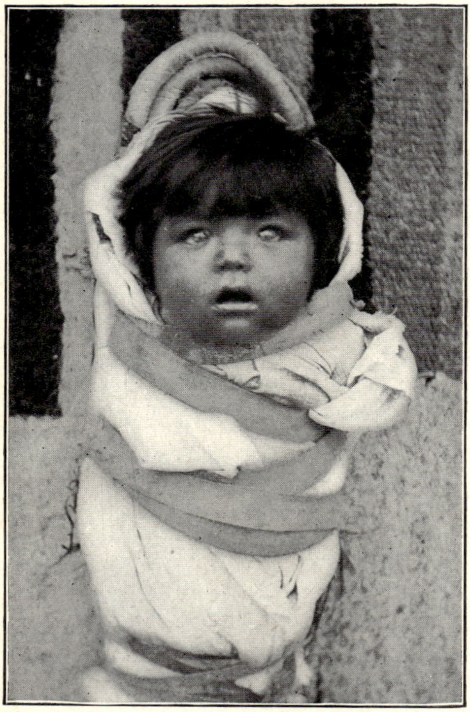

THE BEST NATURED BABY I EVER SAW. HER PARENTS ARE WALLAPAIS.

"The Worden home is sunny and bright, with windows wide open day and night, and the rooms kept always cool and fresh. No useless furniture, no bric-a-brac, no draperies, harbor dust and germs. The walls and hardwood floors and few articles of furniture are kept scrupulously clean, but without ornament. The whole house is given over to the children, and there is no need for prohibitions of any sort.

"Concerning the diet of his children Dr. Worden

says: 'No national or international problems concerning the welfare of our people are as important as our food problem. And yet it is a very simple one, solved by an all-wise Creator before the creation of man. Time enough is wasted in the kitchen of our modern homes, spoiling good food by making almost impossible mixtures and then over-cooking these, to do all the necessary work of any nation. This careless and ignorant diet leads to ill-health, from which there is no escape unless we learn to lead a sensible life, eating moderately of natural foods, and these in simple combinations.

"'With our children, very little cow's milk is used, largely because of its unreliability in the city; but we do not favor an abundance of milk anyway, after children have teeth to use on their food. Their diet consists of fruits, cereals, nuts, and vegetables, no spices, vinegar, etc., being used. Whole wheat flour, the bran included, is used exclusively.

"'They are never urged to eat. We expect them to know whether they are hungry or not. Urging children to eat leads to overfilling of the stomach, and this to bowel disorders, and often death. Next to urging children to eat, as a cause of overeating, is variety. We never supply them with a choice of foods at one meal. The diet for each meal is simple, and yet in one season or year they get quite a variety, as exampled by a list of the fruits they get, one kind at a time: Apples, pears, grapes, plums, cherries, oranges, pineapples, peaches, grape fruit, prunes, apricots, figs, dates, raisins, bananas, melons, and the numerous kinds of berries — all choice fruit. They scorn anything with a bad spot as being not fit to eat. Then again we buy them lots of nuts for food, not just for the fun of cracking and eating and usually overeating. They get nut food as a United States soldier his rations. Next we have an immense choice of vegetables, of which they get one kind at a meal — never two vegetables to one child at the same meal. On such a diet it is no occasion for surprise that they have never been sick. The good health to be derived from a simple meal more than repays for any fancied abstinence.'

"The Worden children are already little athletes. The elder girl is the youngest basket-ball player in Milwaukee. Every evening they exercise for a few minutes nude, incidentally getting an air bath to the skin of the whole body while developing and strengthening the muscles.

"Dr. and Mrs. Worden are not faddists. They are earnestly and steadfastly endeavoring to fulfill the trust committed to them, to develop their children into strong healthy women, to strengthen their powers of endurance, and develop their physical faculties by bringing them up in accordance with all the laws of health."

Another thing that I would have white women learn from their Indian sisters,. is a thing they used to know but are rapidly forgetting. That is, the joy of suckling their own children. An Indian mother that does not suckle her own child is almost unknown. With the "superior classes" of the white race it is the opposite of this proposition that is true. Not only is this of great injury to the child, but it is fraught with most serious consequences to the mother. Is it nothing that the mother of a child willfully puts away from herself all the little, fond, sweet intimacies that naturally grow out of this relationship; the joy of exercise of a natural and beautiful function; the feeling that the baby life is still being sustained by the mother's own life-blood transmuted by mother love and mother-processes into sweet, delicious food that nothing else can equal?

It is a fact that all the higher affections and emotions of the human soul have to be cultivated and

A DILIGENT HOPI BASKET WEAVER, WHO IS ALSO A GOOD MOTHER.

developed. The child sees little or no beauty in a sunset; it must be trained to recognize it. The love of Nature grows as we cultivate it. The nobler emotions of self-sacrifice, humility, kindliness, grow as we cultivate them, and while, where maternity is a perfectly natural process, joy accompanies it in all its manifestations, there is no denying the fact that in our so-called civilization women have to cultivate the feelings connected with the function to bring to themselves the joy they should normally possess. But that there is a joy in suckling one's own child many, many mothers — true mothers — have assured me, and I

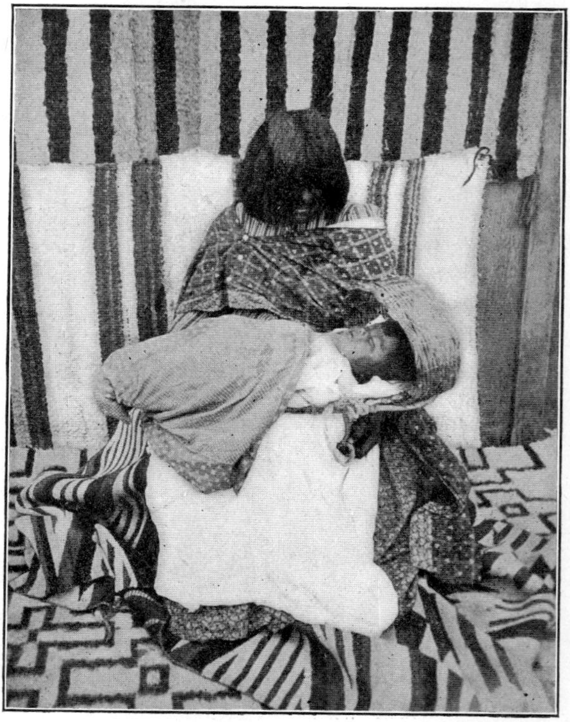

A PROUD AND HAPPY WALLAPI MOTHER.

wish to add my voice to the supplications of the innocent child that every mother give of her own sweet, loving breast to the child she has brought into the world. Some mothers refuse because it destroys the beautiful contour of the bust; others because it demands too close confinement, and would therefore prohibit regular attendance upon club or social functions. Poor women! Bartering their God-given rights and privileges for the messes of pottage that society and club life afford — that is, afford to mothers at the time they should be with their babes. Can any society on earth, any club that ever existed, compensate for the loss of healthful nutrition given from a loving mother's breast? Let the statistics of "bottle-fed" babies attest the dangers that accrue from the mother's refusal (or inability — for which she is to be pitied rather than condemned) to suckle her own young.

A HOPI BABY WHO HAS NEVER YET KNOWN CLOTHES.

CHAPTER XVII

THE INDIAN AND THE SANCTITY OF NUDITY

WHILE adults of both sexes among all Indians wear either a skirt or a gee-string, there is not the slightest hesitancy in allowing the young, both boys and girls, to run about in a state of nudity. Since we have sent white teachers and missionaries to the Indians, they are beginning to learn that somehow—though they can't sort it out just how or why—there is something indecent in allowing nude children to wander about their homes and villages. They are being taught to be "ashamed,"—their children are becoming sex-conscious as are our white children, long before their time, and we are foisting on to them our hateful, impure, and blasphemous conceptions of nudity. For myself I am free to confess that I have no sympathy with this kind of teaching. I think it unnecessary, and not only unnecessary but a positive injury. I believe in the sanctity of nudity, especially in that of young children, and while with our present social customs we cannot allow our children to be nude or partially nude in public, I would that our minds were as clean in this matter as are those of the Indians with whom I have so long been acquainted.

Whatever society may demand of us in public, there is no reason why, in private, both our children and ourselves should not spend a certain portion of every day, if possible, in contact with the direct rays of the sun and the air. Every school in the land should be so equipped, and our children and their parents be so trained, that, under proper direction, a certain part of every day the students could be so exposed. All know the benefit that comes from the exposing of the arms and legs to the sun and breezes at the sea-shore. Men, women, and children alike who flee the city for an annual holiday to the seaside return to their shut-in, civilized (!) life with renewed vigor and health. Why not give some of this life to city children every day in the year? Even in Eastern cities, in winter, a solarium could be created in the top stories of the schoolhouses, and there, with every window wide open, the children clothed in the scantiest of garments, as at the seaside, could go through physical and breathing exercises, and romp or play games for half an hour, to their great benefit both of body and mind.

We have for so long trained ourselves to the half expressed belief that there is something wrong about nudity that we find women's clubs draping statues, and organizations rejecting figures because they are nude, which all ages and all civilized peoples have accepted as pure and chaste works of art. I would not for a moment have it thought that I approve of all nude statues or pictures. Many of them have no virtue to commend them. Yet I would not indiscriminately condemn all works of art in the nude merely because they are nude. We have forgotten the appearance of a healthy body, and feel ashamed to see one. By our mental attitude we accuse the Creator of indecency that "male and female created He them," for, not only do we veil the bodies of the opposite sexes from each other, (which is a perfectly correct and wise thing to do) but daughters are ashamed to be seen nude by their own mothers, and mothers by their daughters. I believe in the sanctity of nudity. Let the sexes remain apart, by all means, but let there be less of false shame when men see nude men, or women see nude women, or either or both see nude children. It is a fact declared by the most conservative of white explorers, that the naked tribes of aborigines are the most pure, chaste, and truly modest. Our conception that because Indians are unclothed they are therefore indecent and unclean, impure and unchaste, is a dirty conception, dishonoring to ourselves and our Creator. *Honi soit qui mal y pense*, and "to the pure all things are pure" are as true to-day as when they were first spoken and written, and while I am as opposed as is any one living to nude pictures and statues that have nothing to commend them but their nudity; while I am strongly opposed to promiscuous nudity either in whole or in part, I am equally opposed to the mental attitude that nudity in itself is wrong, and that the Creator did not know His business when he created us both nude and of different sexes.

A HAVASUPAI CHILD BROUGHT UP TO ENJOY BEING OUT IN THE RAIN.

Benjamin Franklin, John Quincy Adams, and many others of the great men of the world, made it a daily practice to expose their bodies to the sun and the air.

For years I have seized every proper opportunity to do so, such as when I took my fifteen days' rowing trip down the Colorado River. When on the Salton Sea exploring trip; when out in the deserts, the canyons, the forests, on the mountain tops, I endeavored every day to give my body some exposure, and every night and morning, when camping out, before retiring and arising, I have a brief air bath, sometimes with vigorous physical exercises. Thus the power of God's own sun and air enter my body through every pore of the skin, and I enjoy a health, vigor, vim, and tingle of delight I can get in no other way.

When I first visited the Havasupai Indians, all the men were nude, part of the time, save for the breech-clout. In their dances, in some of which I participated, it was a delight to see the movements of their perfect muscles, their bronze flesh glistening in the sun, or in the glow of the camp fires. And men, women, and children all bathed at the same time, in the clear waters of Havasu Creek, all the adults, of course, wearing either a short skirt or a breech clout, but the major part of the body fully exposed. There was no immodesty and no thought of anything of the kind. Nudity or semi-nudity was taken as a matter of course, and neither by word or deed did anyone seem conscious of it. After vigorous swimming, the young men wrestled, the youngsters ran races, the men indulged in various games, their bodies still exposed to the sun and the air, and no one could fail to observe the health, vigor, and robustness that came from this habit of life.

The Hopis train their boys and young men to their morning runs over the desert in a state of almost complete nudity, and in their snake dance races, nothing but the gee-string is worn, and people of both sexes gaze upon them with no thought of immodesty. Modesty is a condition of soul, and has nothing to do with the exposure or covering of the body. One may be a Godiva and be far more modest than another who veils not only her whole body but even her face. And for myself, I wish to record my conviction that it would be far better for the morals of civilized man if he would bring up his children of both sexes to recognize and know the sanctity of nudity, rather than to cover the body as he does and to affirm by his words and suggest by his demeanor that he regards an exposed body as indecent. A small trunk can always be worn and this suffices for every purpose of true modesty.

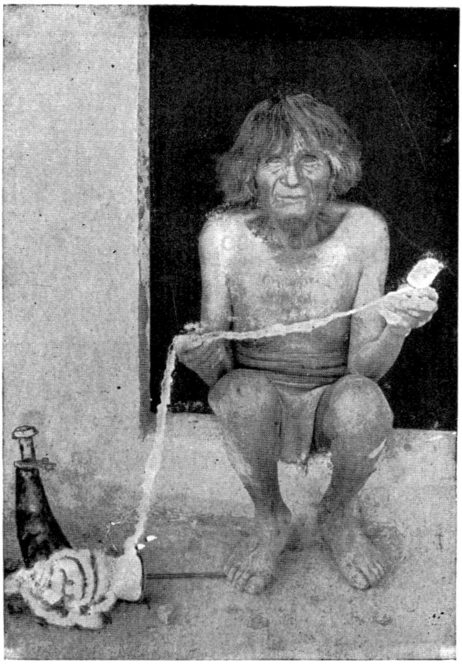

A NUDE HOPI SPINNING WOOL FOR THE MAKING OF A DRESS FOR HIS WIFE.

In many of the leading sanitariums of the world the patients are required to expose their bodies to the sun and air for a certain length of time daily. Here is a struggling to get back to a natural condition, an almost essential condition to the attainment and retention of perfect health. Of the outdoor gymnasiums for men and women at the Boulder

Sanitarium, Colorado, Dr. Howard F. Rand thus writes:

"Here the men patients, clothed with simple trunks, bask in the sunshine on the sand which covers the ground, follow the trainer through the different lines of gymnastic work, finally plunging into the pool and coming out ready to be dried and thoroughly rubbed. Donning their simple apparel, they can, if they choose, proceed up the mountain, and gather beautiful wild flowers and rest the eye on the surrounding scenery.

"The outdoor gymnasium is especially helpful in the treatment of women. It is very difficult to get them to dress properly when taking physical exercise, and they are 'so afraid' of exposing themselves to the sunlight and 'ruining' their complexion. But the beautiful physique of some of our young women who have trained in this line, and the assurance that they can so develop themselves, lead them to make short trips to the gymnasium, and gradually they grow willing to be delivered from close wrappings, and expose themselves to the sunlight. The pleasure is enticing; enjoyment of exercise in this place without the restriction of tight clothing rapidly increases, and desired results are obtained by this means in less time than in any other line of training. The great essential is to have the person in natural condition when exercising, so that all the organs of the body may move freely and naturally, without let or hindrance. Number seems to increase the enchantment; hence the more readily do the timid and backward take the first steps.

"At first it is impossible for many to expand at the waist line; but a jump into the pool, the temperature of the water being 70° to 75°, causes them involuntarily to inflate the respiratory organs, and through this and special training deep breathing becomes habitual in less time than it would in any other way.

"We aim to have our patients spend at least one hour, twice a day (forenoon and afternoon), in the open-air gymnasium.

"Soon after beginning this course, the patient's skin, and mind as well, will be found clearing up. He will say his appetite is better, and that he sleeps more soundly, and is gaining weight and strength. The surface becomes brown in a short time, but as soon as pigmentation ceases, there is a natural, pearly-white hue — a sure indicator of health."

These open-air gymnasiums are to be found at the leading sanitariums of the world, thus clearly showing that the Indian idea of nudity has the sanction of the highest and wisest medical opinions of the white race.

The body is a sweet, a precious, a beautiful expression of God's thought; it was and is intended by the Divine as the house of the mind, the soul, the immortal part of the human being. Paul expressly declares it is "the temple of the Holy Ghost." Every part of it is beautiful, every part God-given. In health it is the most perfect machine ever designed, and the most beautiful. Every function it performs is a marvel, every power contained within it a miracle. How obviously wrong then is anything that disparages, lowers, offends the high and supreme dignity of this glorious structure. Yet we are ashamed of it, we apologize for it, we teach our children to be ashamed of it and to cover it as an evil thing.

CHAPTER XVIII

THE INDIAN AND FRANKNESS

ANOTHER thing the white race might learn from the Indian, and it would be well for them if they did, is the virtue of frankness. If an Indian likes you or dislikes you, he lets you know. There is no pretense, no hypocrisy, and in his speech he indicates his feelings. Then, too, he is not offended by plain speech. If he lies and you tell him so, he honors you; and if you lie, he will not hesitate to say so. Making the fingers of both hands as a tongue on each side of the mouth, he says: "You talk two ways at once," which is Indian for our ruder vernacular: "You are a liar!" There are no conventional lies among Indians. They do not speak untruths for the sake of politeness. They have learned the lesson of the Man of Galilee, who two thousand years ago taught, "Let your yea be yea, and your nay nay, for whatsoever is more than these cometh of evil." Of course there are untruthful Indians, but with the major part their word is never broken. I would just as soon take the simple word of most of the Indians I know as that of the most upright and honored of the old-fashioned Southern gentlemen. And I would no more think of insulting the Indian by putting his integrity in speech on the same plane as that of the ordinary society or business man or woman of America than I would insult the lion by calling him a wolf. Strong words, but true, and capable of demonstration. Too often Indians who come in contact with the whites learn to lie, but the pure, uncontaminated, uncivilized

Indian hates a lie and a liar as much as the proverb says the devil hates holy water. I shall never forget the impression made in the court-room at Flagstaff, Arizona, when Bigwoetten, a Navaho Indian, who had been charged with murder, and who had sent word to the sheriff that it would be useless to hunt for him as he could never be found, but that, if he was wanted, he would come in when the trial began,—I say, I shall never forget the marvelous impression caused by the proud stalking into the court-room of this old and dignified Indian, and his speech to the judge: "Though

THE AUTHOR HAVING A POW-WOW WITH THE YUMA INDIANS.

I am sore wounded, and the journey over the desert has been dreary and long, and has well-nigh killed me, I gave my word that I would be here,— the word of a Navaho that never was broken — so here I am. Do with me as you will, so that you do honestly."

Several times, with perfect confidence, I have risked my life in exploring trips, on the mere word of an Indian that he would be at such a place at a certain time with food and water. And such has been my experience that now I never hesitate to accept the simple word of any Indian who has an ordinarily good reputation.

I have often had pow-wows with various tribes and whatever they have promised me in such councils has invariably been performed.

And yet there is a peculiar twist to the mentality of many Indians that needs comment here. When a stranger is questioning an Indian about anything that she (or he) deems of no great importance, as, for instance, the meaning of a certain design on a basket, the Indian conception of politeness leads her to give you the reply your question seems to call for. For instance, if you see a zigzag design on a basket and you ask her, "Is this to represent lightning?" she thinks that is what you want it to represent, so she says, "Yes!" Ten minutes later and her questioner asks, "Is this the ripple of the sunshine on water?" Again with the same thought uppermost in her mind, that she must be polite to her questioner, that that is the answer asked for, she says, "Yes!" And so on with a dozen different questioners, and all of them with a different interpretation of the same symbol, her answer would be "yes" every time. This, however, is not untruth. It is because the white questioner does not know that his is not the method of extracting truth from an Indian. He has asked for a certain answer and he has it.

CHAPTER XIX

THE INDIAN AND REPINING

IN all my association with Indians, I cannot recall a single instance of repining, regret over the unalterable events of the past, weeping or wailing over joys lost, demoralizing self-pity, or magnified distress because "we have seen better days." The simple, unpretentious, really democratic life of the Indian disposes of these latter ills to which the white race is heir by rendering them impossible, and repining and self-pity seem to have no place in their vocabulary. They weep and wail when their loved ones die; and they gather together and pray if drought or other natural evils destroy their crops, but when the weeping is done it is done, and life's duties are taken up without constant repining or self-pity. What has happened has happened. Nothing can alter it. It is the will of Those Above, or whether it is or not it *IS*, and that is enough. Hence why complain, why protest. Accept the inevitable. Leave it alone. Let the dead past bury its dead. Do the work of to-day; never mind the woe of yesterday.

This seems to me to be the Indian attitude. A kind of proud acquiescence, a manly, womanly recognition of facts, and a willingness to face them and thus triumph over them. Instead of magnifying their sorrows they minimize them by constant labor and by doing the very opposite, viz., magnifying their joys. Often have I heard this done. A widow speaking of her lost husband, and immediately referring in tones of joy to her boys and girls, her fine corn-field, her peach orchard, — her blessings, in fact.

It is simply impossible for any one to estimate the amount of time, strength, energy, and life that have been wasted by the white race in lamenting, repining, weeping, over things that could neither be helped nor changed. And how absurd such lamentation is. If an evil can be remedied, remedy it. If a wrong can be righted, right it. But to waste valuable time, strength, and energy in vain repining and self-pity is a crime that no Indian is so foolish as to commit. It is left to the white race to thus show its superiority! This comes from two or three causes. First: Our race, mainly our women, are not as healthy physically as the Indian, and where physical health is lacking it is so easy to yield to the force of evil circumstance. Strong men or women can force themselves into physical and mental activity and these bring solace and forgetfulness of the pains, ills, and sorrows of the past. Second: The very ease and luxury of our lives which all white people so much covet, give us time and opportunity to sit down and study over sources of sadness, while on the other hand, the Indian woman has her daily work that she must perform, willy nilly, and thus is kept from the contemplation of her sorrows. Third: There is in the Indian that calm serenity of mind and soul that belong only to either very childlike or exceedingly cultured natures. With the Indian it is childlike acceptance of the will of the gods; with Browning, it was the calm philosophy of the highest culture. Unfortunately for most of us, we have lost the religious simplicity of our ancestors, our childlike faith and trust, and have not yet attained to the serenity of the philosopher.

I write this brief chapter merely to call attention to the facts, and to urge upon the white race the necessity, if it would preserve its serenity, of either reverting to the simple faith of the Indian, or of cultivating a religious philosophy that will produce an equal serenity and equanimity in the face of trial, sorrow, misfortune or death.

CHAPTER XX

THE INDIAN AND THE SUPERFLUITIES OF LIFE

THE white race may learn much from the Indian as to the superfluities of life. There is no question but that we — the white race — are cursed with the collecting habit; we are vexed by many possessions. And what is the good of much of what we gather? Mere trash, accumulated for show; bought without much thought merely to gratify a passing whim, and half the time we don't know what to do with our purchases when we have made them. Our *houses* are no longer *homes*, they are converted into bric-a-brac establishments. Our children become a terror to us lest they should touch this or that or the other, and our nervous systems are wrecked because of dread lest our fine "Japanese bowl," or our elegant "Etruscan vase," or our exquisite "Italian figurine," or "that lovely Hindoo idol," should be injured.

A year or two ago I was the guest in the home of an eminent scientist, whose wife is herself a remarkable woman, gifted as a writer and public speaker, and yet whose home is laden with extraneous material to the nerve-breaking point. One evening they were entertaining a well-known author and lecturer, and the hostess had called upon him to tell of some of his interesting experiences. The guest was a normal, healthy man and gentle in his movements, but, while speaking, somewhat free in gesticulation. In one part of his story he made a quick motion and pushed his chair gently back. In doing so he overturned a Japanese vase that stood on a slight pedestal near by. With a crash that shocked the nerves of every one present, the valuable piece of bric-a-brac fell. Fortunately, it was not broken, but, with blanched face, though her voice was well under control, the hostess tenderly picked it up. She endeavored to smooth over the accident, but the author's interest in his story was gone. He brought it to a lame conclusion, and gave an evident sigh of relief, — though quite unconsciously, — when his wife suggested that "the babies might need her presence at home." After they had gone I was witness of the grief and distress of the poor woman who lamented the injury to her treasure, and who evidently valued it far more than she did the comfort and welfare of her visitors and guests.

I sometimes go to homes where the furniture is of the elegantly polished or "enameled" type. To place a book or one's hand upon such polish is to mar the surface. The hostess must either keep the table to be merely looked at, and be in constant terror lest some one outwit her vigilance and mar its "beauty," or resign herself to seeing it used and spoiled.

Now, of all of these things, I constantly ask myself, What 's the use? For myself I value the health and happiness of my wife and my children more than all the bric-a-brac that ever was, or ever will be, made. The nerves of the former, and the healthy, untrammeled movements of the latter, are worth far more than a few "curios." And so with my guests. I want my visitors to feel free to move around and about in my home, as healthy men and women ought to do, and if there is anything in the way of such action the sooner it is knocked down and smashed the better I shall like it. And as for "enameled" furniture: if I found any of it introduced into my house where I was constantly in danger of marring it, I fear my "angry passions would rise," and so would the polished article, to find itself at the next moment on the woodpile. Human happiness and comfort are of more value than many pieces of furniture, and he, and he only, is wise who keeps life as simple as possible, and free from these needless, labor-creating, nerve-wearing luxuries and superfluities of life.

THE WIDOW OF MANUELITO, THE LAST GREAT CHIEF OF THE NAVAHOS. ONE OF THE QUEENLIEST WOMEN IN DIGNITY, GRACE, AND CHARACTER I HAVE EVER MET.

In both men's and women's dress, too, something may be said on this line. The tendency of the age is to add and add and add, until we are burdened by the superfluous. Women want laces, embroideries, tucks, ruffles, pleats, and ribbons; they quilt, braid, hem, and fell to a fearful and wonderful extent, — all adding labor, trouble, and care to life, and depriving them of time that could and should be more wisely and profitably spent. No one loves to see woman or man neater or better dressed than I, but there is a point of simplicity and native dignity beyond which no one can go without getting into the realm of needless, wasteful luxury and harmful superfluity. Some men are as bad as some women, what with ties for every function and hour of the day, cuffs, collars, vests, and creased trousers, all of which must be *a la mode* and *au fait.* To me these things reveal as much *non compos mentis* as they do *a la mode*, for mind should be, *and is*, superior to an excess of such frivolity.

Rose Wood-Allen Chapman in *Good Health* has sagely written upon this subject. She well says:

"The one important thing in life is character; your own character, the character of your husband, your children, your friends. All other things should be judged by their bearing upon this important matter. Things may be delightful in themselves; but if they tend to add to your worries, if they are a barrier between you and your loved ones, if they interfere with the development of the higher faculties of your children, they become undesirable, inadvisable, and should be classed with the superfluities of life.

"The mother who prepares for her baby dainty, hand-made garments, wonderfully trimmed with lace and embroidery, in the majority of instances is depriving that child of personal love and care that rightfully belong to him. What does he care for such finery? He wants his mother's companionship, and for himself perfect freedom for all forms of activity. To so attire him that he must be constantly cautioned, 'Now don't get your dress dirty,' is to interfere with one of his inalienable rights. The wise mother will make her baby's clothes simple, to serve as a background for his infantile charms, instead of taking the attention away from him to center it upon elaborate ornamentation.

"Many housekeepers there are who bemoan their

inability to keep up the interests of their girlhood. They have no time now to play the piano, to read inspiring literature, to join the club, or to enter upon any philanthropic work. They say they feel their deprivation; have they ever tried to see how many of their household tasks could be eliminated as superfluous?

"I have been in homes where there were two and sometimes three pairs of curtains at each window. The effect was rich, but one whose mind was awakened to the question of the superfluities could but think of the extra work such hangings entailed.

"Then there are the 'cozy corners,' the Turkish divans smothered in over-hanging draperies, which the furniture stores are so eager to urge upon their customers as 'the very latest style.' Such corners are gathering-places for dust, and an unnecessary addition to the work of the home.

"Heavy carpets on the floors may feel soft under foot, but they are hard to sweep, are never really clean, save after the annual beating, and so are both unhygienic and burdensome.

"Think how much less drudgery must be performed by the woman who has hard-wood or stained floors with a few medium-sized rugs! Her floors can be wiped up quickly with a damp cloth, and her rugs thoroughly cleaned with a minimum amount of effort.

"At the windows this same woman will have filmy net curtains, with ruffled border, it may be, that are ordinarily cleansed by putting them on the line where the wind can blow the dust out of them; or can easily be laundered when more thorough cleaning is desired.

"On her walls will be a few artistic pictures, with no overhanging festoons or ribbons to catch dust and add to the labor. Bric-a-brac will be conspicuous for its absence; photographs will be put away, instead of covering her dresser and the walls of her bedroom. In a word, her aim will be to have her home light, airy, artistically furnished, but in such a way as to be the least possible burden to her and to her family. Husbands and children find it hard to be careful of the things that have been bought for show. Why not dispense with them, then, and have only that which is necessary and usable?

"Many housekeepers have learned to dispense with unnecessary furnishings, but are still slaves to elaborate meals, especially when they entertain.

"It is wise, in the first place, to remember that the health of the family is conserved by simplicity in the meals. Even though they are now used to a larger variety at each meal, they can be gradually accustomed to a simple diet. No soup when there is dessert and no dessert when there is soup, is a very good rule for dinner. The other course should consist of a meat substitute and only two vegetables. A simple breakfast food, with bread and butter and fruit, is enough for the morning meal; while an equally simple supper should be entirely satisfactory.

"It is a temptation to leave the paths of simplicity when company is coming; but if we just remember that our friends come to see us, not to eat our food, we will find it easier to restrain our inclinations in this direction. Oftentimes housewives become possessed with a spirit of emulation which leads Mrs. Smith to feel that she must set forth a more elaborate meal than Mrs. Jones had served, while Mrs. Robinson in turn strives to eclipse Mrs. Smith, and as a result meals become so complicated as to be most burdensome to the hostess and almost dangerous to the guests. Let us confine our efforts to making our simple entertainment as attractive as possible, and furnishing such wit and merriment therewith, such geniality and kindliness, as shall make our guests feel that they have partaken of a feast."

I have already, in other chapters, commented upon some of these things, as revealed in the light of the Indian's life. Their lives are, perforce, models of simplicity, devoid of luxuries and also of superfluities. It is not my intent to suggest that we should revert to their method of living a simple and unluxurious life, but I do long with all my heart that we might take lesson from them, and find the golden mean between their life and our too complex and superfluity-laden life. If health and happiness are the ends to be attained in life *they*, with their rude simplicity, have surpassed us, with our elegant and ornate complexity. And for me and mine I prefer health and happiness rather than all the superfluities that a commercially-cursed, bargain-counter, curio-loving, bric-a-brac adoring, showy, shoddy civilization can give.

CHAPTER XXI

THE INDIAN AND MENTAL POISE

ON a trip made recently from Yuma to the Salton Sea, down the overflow of the Colorado River, I found occasion to watch my two Indians in contrast with four white men of more than ordinary intelligence and ability. In some important things the Indians lost nothing by the comparison. Indeed, several times

CAMPING OUT ON THE WAY TO THE SALTON SEA.

I called the attention of my white companions to them, and to certain characteristics which are by no means confined to them, but that belong to most Indians, and urged their emulation. Some of these will form the subject of this chapter.

One member of my party was a "reverend"—a missionary. He was a fine, open-hearted fellow whom we all liked, but every once in a while — indeed, I ought to say frequently — he would make suggestions to the Indian to go here, or go there, which finally called

JIM, OUR YUMA INDIAN BOATMAN.

forth (from me) a forceful rebuke. Let me explain the situation fully. When we came to the place where the Colorado River left its banks and entered a mesquite forest, its waters were naturally much divided. As we did not know where each current led, and how soon it would spread so as to render further progress in our boats impossible, it was a situation that called for great knowledge as to determining the course of the best and deepest current, and quick decision; for, as we were carried along among mesquites, a few moments of indecision meant being thrust into a mesquite tree, perhaps, where cruel thorns spared no one, because of his indecision. Reader, do you know what a mesquite is? Its proper name should be "me scratch." If you come within ten feet of one it verily seems to reach out for you and scratch you somewhere. Imagine your thorniest rosebush multiplied by fifty and all concentrated and condensed into one tree with thorns much longer, far more pointed, and with poison lurking on the end of them, and you have a not very much exaggerated idea of the mesquite. Now to have our missionary friend bawling out all the time, "Better go this way," or "Better go that," was both annoying and useless, so I finally told him I had brought the Indian because I knew that he knew a thousand-fold more of such a current and how to get through this wilderness of mesquite than I did. "And," said I, "as far as I am concerned, I should feel it was an impertinence for me to make even a suggestion to the Indian. He *knows* where I *guess*, and yet as you know, I have had far more experience in this kind of thing than you have. Don't you think it wiser for you to add a little more silence to your possessions?"

He was, as I have said, a royal-hearted fellow, and he took my rebuke in a manly, Christian way, for a few moments' reflection showed him that what I said was wisdom.

Now, while these wild and foolish suggestions were being made to the Indian, what did he do? It was most interesting to me to watch him. Instead of replying and arguing with a lot of vehement words, he smiled quietly, looked at me to see if I approved of the suggestion, and when he saw my absolutely impassive face, went on following his own course. Had he been a white man — or like most white men — he would have shouted back that he was going some other way, or called his adviser a fool, or informed him that he knew his business, or some other equally agreeable thing.

This serenity of mind in the Indian is often called impassiveness or stolidity. It shows how little the

IN THE BOATS, IN THE RAIN, ON OUR WAY TO THE SALTON SEA.

critics have known of the Indian to speak thus. They are as sensitive as children, morbidly so sometimes, but they have the self-control not to show it, and in matters like this, where they are sure their knowledge is superior to that of their adviser, they go on with a proud disregard of criticism or censure.

This calmness was also shown in the face of danger. Several times we came to places where there was both difficulty and danger. We had three boats. In the first were Jim (the Indian) and myself, seeking out the way; in the second, Indian Joe and Mr. Louis Francis Brown (business manager of the Burton Holmes lectures); and in the third his reverence and two others. When we came to the thrilling places, Jim soon learned that he was to take the responsibility, save where there was time and opportunity to discuss matters with me, and with a dignified self-reliance he made his choice, and then awaited results. If they were unpleasant, as they often were, there was no murmuring, no shouting, no remonstrance. He took things as they came, and made the best of them. The second boat followed, and there was little more said there than in our boat; but from the third came a constant babble of voices, cries to do this or that, shouts of warning, remonstrance, and fault-finding. I could not help contrasting the demeanor of the Indians with that of the civilized whites, and wishing that the latter could and would learn the lesson so clearly taught.

The quickness of Jim's observations and his decisions were remarkable, and I wished my children, and others too, might have gone to school to him for a year or two. He saw where the sand bars were that I could not see; he could tell which way the wind was blowing, when to me it seemed to be blowing several directions at once; he was generally able to tell where the largest amount of water was flowing, and only two or three times did he make a mistake so that we had to turn back. And when those times came, there was no grumbling, no murmuring, no finding fault. He accepted the disagreeable inevitable just as easily and readily as he accepted the pleasant.

This silence and serenity in the face of annoyances is a very pleasing feature of Indian life to me. What is the use of fault-finding and complaining over disagreeable things that cannot be helped? I have just had an example (and he is but one of scores that occur to my mind) of the opposite spirit shown by a very proud and haughty member of the white race. We were on the car together, coming from the East. The first time he had a meal in the dining-car he came back furious: the chicken was cooked two or three days ago, and was weeks old to begin with; all the provisions were equally bad, the service was abominable, and the charges infamous. Then the speed of the train came in for censure. They did things differently on the New York Central or the Pennsylvania, (forgetful of the fact that those roads run through thickly populated centers, and have a passenger patronage ten times as large as is possible to the western railways that pass through unsettled and barren regions). Then, though it was perfectly delicious weather, he had to kick against its being warm and disagreeable, and so on *ad libitum* until I was sick of him, as was everybody else in the car. In twenty-six years of association with the Indians, I never met with one such disagreeable grumbler. The white race retains that characteristic practically to itself. If things are disagreeable and can be changed, the Indian calmly and deliberately goes to work to change them. If they are unchangeable he serenely and silently bears them. It is more manly, more agreeable, more philosophical.

Time and again I have had white men with me on various trips who needed to learn this simple and useful lesson. They made of themselves intolerable nuisances by their whining, whimpering, and complaining. Those of my readers who care to read Chapter XV in my "In and Around the Grand Canyon," and the story of the Britisher on page 18 and onward in "The Indians of the Painted Desert Region," will see that I know that of which I speak. And these are but two experiences out of many similar ones. Yet I have been with Indians again and again in places of distress, deprivation, and danger, and in all my experiences have not heard a half hour's unpleasant words. Once I started to explore a series of side canyons of the great Grand Canyon. My guide was Sin-ye-la, an intelligent Havasupai. We had a most arduous trip; ran out of water and food; our horses gave out and we had to catch, saddle, and ride unbroken steeds, and finally he caught a wild mule upon which we placed the pack. The horrors and anguish of that trip I have never written, yet there was not a suggestion of complaining from Sin-ye-la, until I decided to leave the canyons and go across the desert to a certain spot where he did not wish to accompany me. Even then he merely stated his case with little or no argument and when I proved obdurate, refused to accompany me, and in fifteen minutes we parted, good friends, he to go his way and I mine.

Another time, as recorded in my Canyon book, I was caught in a marble trap with Wa-lu-tha-ma, where it seemed impossible that we could ever escape. The Indian's calmness was almost too much. He was almost as resigned as a Mahommedan who believes in Fate. Yet, though I remonstrated with him for his despairing attitude so that we eventually got out, I believe I would rather have that bravery of despair which dares to face death without complaining or whimpering, than the fault-finding, "Why did you bring me into such dangers?" or "Shall I ever get out of this horrible place?" that some white men indulge in.

WALUTHAMA, MY HAVASUPAI GUIDE.

When, on the Salton trip, we came to the beginning of the most dangerous part where I had been told we should go "fifty miles in fifty minutes," and there were many rapids which would dash our boats to pieces, and where undermined cliffs, forty, fifty, and more feet high, were likely to be suddenly precipitated into the river, and might fall upon us and our boats and send us to instant destruction; when I told my Indian of these dangers he calmly looked me in the eye and answered my question, "You afraid to go, Jim?" with a counter question: "You afraid?" And when I said "No," and answered his further "You swim?" with a "Yes!" he immediately replied; "All right, I go."

Of course I do not wish for one moment to suggest that this virtue of courage is not the white man's. For love of home and country white men will go to death with a smile on their lips. But in work which the world does not see, where men are simply paid two dollars a day wages, to face danger and possible death as a matter of course, this I have found rare with the white man, and very common with an Indian. The facing of danger and death is part of their every-day life. It calls for the exercise of no special virtues. Strong in body, daring in mind, fearless in soul, duty must be done and done unhesitatingly, regardless of whether danger or death are lurking near. I am free to confess this large bold faith in life and the Supreme pleases me. The man who is always seeking to guard his own life, who refuses to run any risks, who never goes except where all is safe, may be a more comfortable man to live with, but as for me, I prefer the spirit of the man who dares and trusts; the man who does the unsafe things because it is his duty to do them, and who faces death and thinks nothing of it. The man who is prodigal of his strength and courage and faith is the man who saves them. The man who is constantly watchful lest he overdo, who refuses to run any risks, who would rather run away than dare, is the one who, in the end, will be found short in manhood and worthy accomplishment.

So I emulate the Indian in these things, and seek to be like him. This prodigality and strength in work calls for more comment. Labor unions are making one of the greatest mistakes of their career in restricting the full exercise of a man's energy. In limiting his daily output they are bucking against that which every man should strive to possess, viz., the spirit of prodigal energy in work. My Indian would row all day, and after a few hours of especially hard work I would ask if I might not relieve him. "No; like 'em," was his reply invariably. He liked his work. It was a joy to him. What was the result? A body of tested steel; lungs equal to every demand; muscles that responded to every strain; eyes as clear as stars; brain quick and alert because of a healthy body made and kept so by hard, continuous labor. We are told that the Indians are lazy. It is not true. Some few may be; but the Indians of the Southwest do their work heartily and well, and with a prodigal energy that is as novel and startling to most white men as it is educative and suggestive to them. As for me, I have learned the lesson. When I reach a station and have time, I walk to my hotel, and refuse to allow any one to carry my usually heavy grips. I seek for the physical exercise. Many a time I arrange for an arduous exploring trip in order to compel myself to great exertions. I know that when I get started I must go on, and in the going on, though I get very weary, I know I am developing power and hoarding up health, energy, and strength for future use. A few weeks ago I started with a comrade for a few hundreds of miles of tramping and riding over the Colorado Desert, up mountain trails, through waterless wastes. My part of the journey was shortened by circumstances over which I had no control, but my assistant and artist took the whole trip, arduous and exhausting though it was, and I envied them and regretted my inability to go along.

Another thing my Indian helpers have taught me. That is a prompt readiness to obey in any service they have agreed to perform, or anything that comes legitimately in the course of their work. There is no holding back, no remonstrance, no finding fault, no crying out that they were not engaged to do this. They perform the service, not only without a murmur, but with a ready willingness that is delightful in this age when every one expects a tip for the slightest service. This comes from two things, viz., a strong, healthy body which responds willingly to any ordinary demands upon it, and a healthy state of mind which neither resents service nor wishes to measure every expenditure of energy in a monetary balance. We are making a grand mistake in basing our present-day civilization upon material wealth. "What is there in it for me?" should be more than a query applying to mere cash. What is there in it of service, of helpfulness to my fellow-man, of healthfulness to myself, of increase of my own strength and power. The men who are relied upon by employers and by the nation are not the men who have selfishly sought their own monetary gain. There is no doubt that such seekers often seem to gain and do really gain a temporary advantage; but it is not a real advantage. It is an advantage of pocket gained at a loss of manhood, physical, mental, and spiritual, and that man who is not worth more in body, mind, and soul than his pocket can never be much of a man.

CHAPTER XXII

THE INDIAN AND SELF-RESTRAINT

FEW of the superior white race would think of looking to the Indian for examples of self-restraint, but I can give them here one of the most marked examples in history. Before the advent of the white man in America the various aboriginal tribes roamed over the plains, the mountains, the foothills, and in the forests, and with snare and trap, gin and bow and arrow caught or slew the game needed for food. These tribes were often hostile to each other; they trespassed on each other's hunting-grounds, and in consequence, often fought in deadly wars which came nigh to exterminating some of them. They were not regardful, therefore, one would think, of the rights or needs of others than themselves to the game they hunted; and it is absurd (so the school-books would tell us) to assume that they would be provident or careful to preserve game for the future. Hence they would slay ruthlessly (the same authorities would doubtless declare), indifferent as to the days to come and their future needs, merely seeking food for to-day, and gorging upon it to repletion. In this case, however, the school-books would be wrong. In the hundreds or thousands of years that the Indians controlled this great continent they never once "killed out" any one of their hunting-fields.

When the white race appeared upon the scene, game of every kind,— fish, flesh, and fowl,— was plentiful. Trappers and hunters went up and down the rivers, where beaver and otter, musk and mink, lived, and through the forests where birds nested and deer, antelope, and other game browsed; climbed the mountains where bear and puma lodged, and ever their bales of skins, furs, peltries, and hides loaded the canoes and the decks of returning vessels. Here was the best proof of the Indian's self-restraint and provident foresight for the future, in that the white man found such an abundance of all kinds of game ready to his hand.

Then came the master mind of an Astor who valued money more than the future. What did it matter to him that game of a hundred kinds disappeared from the face of the earth provided he could make a fortune? What cared he that men and women would starve in the days to come so long as he could pile up his hoard of pelts, and sell them to add to his wealth? Modern commercialism, that damned and damning spirit of our civilization that sees nothing but dollars, that would shut out the glory of the sun rather than miss the ten-cent piece close at hand, entered into the game. Then the sportsman and the pot hunter of the white race came also, and between them and the Buffalo Bills who shot down buffaloes by the thousand for food to supply the builders of the transcontinental railways, in half a generation they cleared the prairies of the millions of noble buffaloes which used to roam in vast herds, left nothing but slender bands or solitary animals of the moose and elk, and drove these into almost inaccessible solitudes for self-preservation, and nearly stripped the country of deer, antelope, wild turkeys, and sage hens. Then they passed laws to protect "game," making a close season so that the Indians, who, in their days of freedom and wildness, needed no law but their own good sense and self-restraint, cannot now shoot at all save in the few days when the restrictions are removed. So that, practically speaking, the Indian now has no hunting-ground; he is debarred from obtaining wild game for food for himself and family, and all because of the infernal greed and equally infernal brutality of the pot-hunter. Here, then, is a national proof — for what I have said is practically true of every state in the country — that the white race has much to learn of self-restraint from the despised Indian. Self-restraint as to greed,— for, until the advent of the white, one Indian never sought to build up mere wealth at the expense of or to the injury or detriment of his fellows. This was the white man's way, not his! He practised self-restraint, for the Indians knew and realized that if the animals were killed too closely the species would soon become extinct, and future generations, if not themselves, have to suffer.

To most people the Indian is a careless creature, content if his belly is filled to-day, improvident for the future, and therefore unwise, unthoughtful, and to be condemned. May it not be in this apparent carelessness for the future the Indian is wiser than we, that he is deliberately exercising a beneficial restraint? Think of the wild hurly-burly of our struggle to accumulate, and then consider the expense, the worry, the endless care of protecting that which we have accumulated. One far wiser than the sages of to-day once declared that we were to "take no thought for the morrow," and in His whole teaching and life reprobated the struggle for wealth, and the life of selfish ease that comes with its attainment.

One of the greatest curses of our present age and

civilization is love of ease, craving for luxury, desire to "have a good time." We worship money because it brings these things, forgetful of the teachings of history that luxury and ease beget sensuality and vice, and these in turn beget disease, decay, and death. I am opposed to great money-getting on this account, and would not amass a fortune if I could. As for leaving large sums of money to my children, especially my sons, nothing could ever induce me to do it. If much money should ever come to me I hereby serve notice upon all concerned that I shall spend it, wisely and usefully, as my best judgment dictates, as soon as I can, and anyhow get rid of it so that no son of mine shall say that the money I left him helped him on the downward path.

The Indian knows well the lesson that physical health comes only by the exercise of the body, therefore he definitely refuses any course of life that would prevent it; he welcomes for himself, his wife, his sons, and his daughters physical work; he also knows that mental and spiritual improvement come only by the exercise of mental and spiritual faculties, and he shuns everything that stultifies them. Did he know English, he could sing with Thomas Gray:

> "From toil he wins his spirits light,
> From busy day the peaceful night:
> Rich, from the very want of wealth,
> In heaven's best treasures, peace and health."

And he puts into practical life what another of our sages well expressed when he said: "Occupation and exercise are the hand-maidens of purity and strength." Too often we merely read these wise words. The Indian lives them. In this the white race can well imitate him. He faces hardship and danger with eagerness that thereby he may develop courage and strength. He takes his sons and punishes them in what we should call a cruel manner to develop fortitude; he sends them out into the desert, mountain, and forest solitudes that there they may meet and talk with Those Above. Every youth or young man who hopes to be a "medicine man" goes out to some such solitary place. He takes no food, no nourishment of any kind, and fasts several days and nights. He drinks nothing but a little water. He sleeps as little as possible. Then if spirits come to him he must obey the teachings and requirements of each one. These teachings and requirements demand the suppression of the natural instincts and desires, and the exercise of positive restraints to an extent that the greatest religious devotee of the white race would scarcely be willing to submit to. One spirit demands that water be drank but once a day, no matter how hot the weather; another that no food shall be taken on three days out of each week; another that no hide shall be made into moccasins, and so on. This, therefore, means a life of self-denial and restraint that surpasses anything known in civilization. Our Catholic priests take a vow of perpetual chastity and obedience, the members of the religious orders go further and pledge themselves to perpetual poverty, but these Indian medicine men, who accept the aid of many spirits, — ten, twenty, and even thirty, — are limited and restricted in their lives to a degree that is as astonishing as it is, to the majority of the white race, unknown.

Now, while the specific acts of restraint of the Indian may not appeal to me, *the spirit of them* is much needed by our whole race. Self-restraint, self-denial, self-control, are the bulwarks of spiritual power. He only is strong in spirit who can control himself, hence I would that the white race would learn these lessons from the Indian.

Browning thoroughly believed in this spirit of self-restraint, self-sacrifice, self-control. In his Rabbi Ben Ezra he preaches some strong doctrines. Nothing is more needed to-day than the following robust and forceful words put into practical every-day living:

> "Then, welcome each rebuff
> That turns earth's smoothness rough,
> Each sting that bids, not sit, nor stand, but go!
> Be our joys three parts pain,
> Strive and hold cheap the strain,
> Learn, never mind the pang; dare, never grudge the throe!"

CHAPTER XXIII

THE INDIAN AND AFFECTATION

MOST people of the white race may learn from the Indian in the matter of affectation. Few of us are simple and natural in our social manners. My own family often joke me, when, in answering the telephone, I respond in what they call my "dressy tone." The other day a lady, whose husband is a college professor, mistook me for a distinguished eastern psychologist whose surname happens to be the same as mine. Until she discovered her mistake she "minced and mouthed" in a most ludicrous fashion (how I wish she could have seen herself as I saw her!) merely because she thought I was a prominent man in the field wherein her husband was a more humble member. The criticism on my own "dressy tone" is a perfectly just one. I find myself, often, "putting on style" because I want to appear "my best." After due consideration I have decided to confess that — like most people — I have a variety of "celluloid smiles" which unconsciously I put on or off as occasion requires. We are not simple, not natural in our relationships one with another. We feel that we must "make an impression," that we must "appear well." The result is we are unnatural, affected, often deceptive, and many a time disagreeable. Affectation in speech and manner is always a sign of mental meanness, — of what is commonly called vulgarity, and is never to be commended but is always to be condemned.

On the other hand, if the President of the United

APACHE INDIAN WHO REFUSED TO "PUT ON STYLE" TO PLEASE THE WHITE MAN.

States were to visit a tribe of uncontaminated Indians, as, for instance, the Navahos, they would treat him in exactly the same manner as they would the humblest citizen; except, of course, that if the president asked for a pow-wow they would give him one, and treat his words with respectful deference. But there would be no affectation in their dealings with him, no putting on of airs or style. With frank, open directness, with the respect they show, as a rule, to each other, and no more, they would listen to all he had to say and give hearty and manly response of approval or disapproval. They have no "company manners," no changes of voice which are used according to the social status of the listener. There are no snobs among them. "A man's a man for a' that," no matter whether he wears an old army overcoat and a top hat or merely a tight skin and his gee-string.

The white race, too, is fearfully affected in its pretense at knowing more than it can know. We are all ashamed to say, "I don't know!" I believe this applies more truthfully to women than to men. Since the era of the woman's club, the gentle sex has been wild to accumulate knowledge, and sadly too often, it is content to *appear* to have the knowledge rather than appear ignorant. One has but to look over the programs of a score or a hundred women's clubs, as I have recently done, to see proof of this in the vast range many of them take *in a single season.* They crowd into an hour's or two hours' session what no person living can get a reasonable grasp of in less than from three months to a year of fairly consistent and persistent study. They jump from "The Romantic School of Music," one week to "The Effect of the Renaissance upon Gothic Art," the next, and the third week finds them swallowing a concentrated pill on "The Poets of the Victorian Era," while on the fourth they completely master all that can be learned of "The Franciscan Mission Epoch in California and Its Influence upon the Indians."

Yet let it not be thought that I am not a believer in education for women, women's clubs, and the like. I believe in everything that *really helps.* And if these clubs would compel mental exercise enough to give a fair grasp of *one subject a year*, they would be doing work of incalculable benefit. But this smattering of knowledge, this thin spreading out of scraps of information, feed no one's mind, and the pretense that comes from an assumed knowledge does the mind and soul of the pretender more harm than a dozen clubs can eradicate in a lifetime. Hence, let us become simple-minded, as the Indians. They "don't know," and they know they don't know, and they are willing to say so.

There is another affectation to which I must refer. We Americans pretend to be democratic, yet we have a caste of wealth that is more disgusting, degrading, and demoralizing than the Hindoo castes, or the social scale of European aristocracy. We "kow tow" to an English lord as if he were a little god, and we bow and scrape and mince our words when we come in contact with the *nouveau riche* of our own land, just as if they were made of different material from ourselves. The space given in our newspapers to the most trivial doings of Alice Roosevelt, both before and after she married Congressman Longworth; the recital of the actions of the "society" few,— the Vanderbilts, Astors, Goulds, Carnegies, Harrimans, Fishes, and the rest, — are proofs of our affected snobbism.

THE INDIAN AND AFFECTATION

I have not yet attained to the mental serenity and calm philosophy of the Indian, but I am seeking it, where I shall judge all men and women not by their exterior circumstances of wealth, position, dress, or birth, but by inherent character, perfection of body, force of mind, and beauty of soul.

CHAPTER XXIV

THE INDIAN AND ART WORK

EVEN our artists and designers may learn much of great importance from the Indian. While to most of my readers it may come as a surprise that I claim great artistic powers for the Indian, yet no one can carefully study the basketry and pottery of the Amerind and not know the perfect justice of the claim. In my larger work on this subject * I have fairly discussed the ability of the Indians in this regard; and to those who are not aware of the vast debt the white race owes to the aboriginal woman in artistic as well as other lines, I earnestly commend a perusal of that masterly work by a conscientious and thorough student, Otis T. Mason, of the Smithsonian Institution, entitled "Woman's Share in Primitive Culture."

In reference to their basketry, however, more than a mere passing mention is required. The Indian weaver shows marvelous ability in the creation of form, color, stitch, and design. Turning to Nature for her original inspirations she is not a mere copyist of what others have done. All her forms are based upon utility, and therefore meet the first and highest requirement of all art when applied to articles that are to serve a useful purpose, viz., adaptation to use. There is no reversal of principles in manufacture, as is so often the case with white workers who value appearance, so-called ornament, finish, etc., rather than adaptation to purpose or utility. Wherever anything is allowed to usurp the place of this primary element, the work is

* Indian Basketry and How to Make Indian and Other Baskets.

doomed even before it is made. On the other hand, frankness, honesty, simplicity, directness, characterize the manufactures of the Indian. They are to serve such and such a purpose; that purpose is openly denoted. The result is that, to the unperverted eye,

ONE OF THE FINEST YOKUT BASKETS IN EXISTENCE.

the artistic work of the unspoiled Indian is as perfect in form as it can be. There is no wild straining after unique effect; no fantastic distortions to secure novelty; everything is natural and rational, and therefore artistically effective.

In color, too, the original work of the Indian weavers, before the vile aniline dyes were forced upon them by the "civilized" and "Christian" traders and missionaries, was above criticism. The old baskets and blankets are eagerly sought after, at fabulous prices, by the most refined and critical of artists and connoisseurs because of the perfection of their color harmonies. In every good collection are to be seen such specimens that are both the admiration and despair of modern artists.

As for weave, it is asserted upon the highest authority that there is not a weave or stitch known to modern art that was not given to our civilization by the aborigines. And they have many stitches of great effectiveness that we have not availed ourselves of. Take the Pomas alone — a tribe of basket-makers who live in northern California. They have not less than fourteen different stitches or weaves, some of them of marvelous beauty and strength. In one of the accompanying pictures is a specimen of their carrying baskets. This basket will hold a large load of seeds or fruit, and when so laden requires a construction of great durability to sustain the burden. It is woven with this express purpose in view, yet it is artistically decorated with a beautifully worked out design. Here is an important lesson the white race might learn, viz., that the utensils of daily life should be surrounded with as much beauty as is practical. The kitchen should be as full of enjoyment to the eye, in reason, as the parlor. The cook and maid need æsthetic surroundings as well as — indeed, more than, — the mistress and her children. If social custom insists upon making servants of one part of its members, the other part should be willing to make their "servitude" as comfortable and beautiful

vated" audience upon this subject of Indian designs that have a personal meaning, and when I got through I heard one highly civilized and cultivated man exclaim in disgust: "Why, he'll soon try to make us believe that our own wall-paper patterns ought to mean something!"

A CHEMEHUEVI BASKET OF BEAUTIFUL FORM AND DESIGN.

Most certainly I will! The idea that we, the superior, the wise race, use designs in our goods that are supposed to be beautiful to us, and yet that have no meaning! What absurdity and foolishness for our girls and women to spend hours on "fancy-work" (!), the designs of which are a crazy, intricate something to be dreaded rather than admired. The Indians have more sense than to waste their time over such foolishness. They have studied Nature in all her varying forms, and their minds are stored up with a thousand and one designs which they can transfer at pleasure to their basketry, pottery, or blanketry. I have had the pleasure of teaching this basic principle

BASKET BOWL MADE BY PALATINGWA WEAVER.

of art work to many white women, and I learned it from the Indian. One woman wanted to get a design for her sofa pillows. I asked her if she had no flowering vine over her porch. She said "Yes." "Then copy its leaf and flower," was my reply, and when she did so, and saw the beauty of the design she had *created* from Nature, her soul was filled with a new joy, and she wrote me that few things had given her more pleasure than the discovery of that basic principle.

Think of the white race making baskets. Where do they go to for their forms and designs? In thousands of cases they take my own books and copy from them! But where did I get them? I am no creative artist, no inventor of design! I got them, "body, soul, and breeches," from the Indian,— every one of them; and yet the "superior race" must go to them to copy, instead of so disciplining the powers of observation from Nature that designs for embroidery, for basketry, for fancy-work of every description, are contained within their own memories. The Indian's life has trained these wonderful faculties of observation and memory. He was compelled to watch the animals in order that he might avoid those that were dangerous and catch those that were good for food; to follow the flying birds that he might know when and where to trap them and secure their eggs; the fishes as they spawned and hatched; the insects as they bored and burrowed; the plants and trees as they grew and budded, blossomed and seeded. He became familiar, not only with such simple things as the movements of the polar constellations and the retrograde and forward motions of the planets, but also with the less known spiral movements of the whirl-winds as they took up the sands of the desert; and the zigzags of the lightning were burned into his consciousness and memory in the fierce storms that, again and again, in darkest night, swept over the exposed area in which he roamed; with the flying of the birds, the graceful movements, the colors, and markings of the snakes, the peculiar wigglings of insects, and their tracks, and those of reptiles, birds, and animals, whether upon the sand, the snow, the mud, or more solid earth, he soon became familiar. The rise and fall of the mountains and valleys, the soaring spires and wide-spreading branches of the trees, the shadows they cast, and the changes they

AN EXQUISITELY WOVEN YOKUT BASKET SHOWING ORIGIN OF ST. ANDREW'S CROSS, FROM THE DIAMOND OF THE RATTLESNAKE.

underwent as the seasons progressed, the scudding or anchored clouds in their infinitude of form and color, the graceful arch of the rainbow, the peculiar formation and dissipation of the fogs, the triumphant lancings of the night by the gorgeous fire-weapons of the morning sun, the stately retreat of the king of day as evening approached, — all these and a thousand and one other things of beauty in Nature the Indian soon learned to know, and from all these mental images he can readily draw when a design is needed.

Is it not well that the white race should learn to observe the things of Nature? We have a few nature writers: Thoreau, John Burroughs, Olive Thorne Miller, Elizabeth Grinnell, John Muir, Ernest Seton Thompson, Wm. J. Long, and Theodore Roosevelt, but why should we need nature books? We have the whole field of Nature for our own; every page is open to us, and the need of these books is proof that we have not, and do not, take the trouble to read Nature for ourselves. The Indian does better than this. He is a personal student. He finds joy and mental development in the results of his own observation, and until the white race learns his lesson, it will be behind him in its joy in Nature, its wisdom gained from Nature, in the physical health, vigor, and strength that Nature always gives to her devotees, and in the true art development that alone can come from familiarity with Nature in all her varying moods.

CHAPTER XXV

THE INDIAN AND RELIGIOUS WORSHIP

THE DIGNIFIED AND SOLEMN ROW OF SNAKE PRIESTS IN THE HOPI SNAKE DANCE CEREMONIES.

ANOTHER thing that the civilized of this age may well learn from the Indian is intense earnestness and sincerity in all matters of religion. It is a painful thing for me to go into many of our city churches. Well-dressed women and girls and young men will sit and whisper through even the most sacred parts of the service. Indeed, it is the exception, not the rule, that I ever go to a service without being outraged by some such exhibition of rudeness, ill manners, and irreverence. This kind of thing is unknown with the Indian. Religion is a serious thing. Fun is fun, and when he goes in for fun he does it with thoroughness and completeness; but when his religious instincts are called upon, he puts aside all fun, and enters into the spirit of the occasion with becoming reverence and solemnity. It is civilized people who go into churches of other faiths than their own and gape and "gawp" around, whispering the while to one another at the strange things they see. Protestants are particularly guilty of this serious vice. Roman Catholics are so trained to attend to their own devotions, and *to be devout* in the house of God, that they pay no attention to one another, but Protestants will go to a Catholic church, or one of some other denomination than their

HOPI INDIANS AT THEIR FLUTE CEREMONIES. THIS IS A PRAYER FOR WATER TO FLOW INTO THEIR DESERT SPRINGS.

own, and behave in a manner that I would never insult the Indians by calling "savage" or "uncivilized." An Indian will not even set foot on the top of one of the underground kivas where religious ceremonies of one clan are going on to which he does not belong. I do not ignore the fact that this reserve comes from superstitious fear lest some harm befall him, and this fear, perhaps, is not good. But whether from fear or not, the reverence for the sacred place and the ceremonies going on is refreshing and gratifying. Especially so is it to me after seeing, week after week, a crowd of so-called civilized young men (and old) lounging around a church door, sometimes smoking, making comments upon the people entering the church. I have as little toleration for the acts of these young men who thus selfishly rob people of their comfort and destroy their religious feeling as I would have for any one who would laugh at sorrow, or make a mock of

THE CHIEF PRIEST OF THE ANTELOPES MARCHING TO THE DANCE PLAZA.

the grief of the bereaved. And my feeling extends also to the officials of the church who will permit such outrageous conduct. Churches are for the education of all the people in religious and higher things. How can youth be educated in higher things when the very precincts of the church are allowed to be used by them for acts of discourtesy, rudeness, and selfish disregard for the thoughts and rights of others? With the Indians these things never occur. In looking at ceremonies in which they have no part, their manner betokens the profoundest respect and reverence. If not for the worship itself, it is yet shown to the feelings of those who do worship. I have photographs in my

THE CIRCUIT OF ANTELOPE PRIESTS BEFORE THE KISI IN THE HOPI SNAKE DANCE.

collection of Indian youths standing at the door of a Christian church while the priest within intoned the mass, or performed some part of the appointed ritual. The rapt expression of intent earnestness and seriousness is so far removed from the flippant, indifferent, careless expression and attitude of many young men of my own race that I long for the latter to know something of the feeling and reverence of the former.

Then in the religious ceremonies in which they take part, their demeanor is remarkable in its intent seriousness and earnestness. I have seen Indians at their shrines, when they thought they were entirely alone, pray with an agony of seriousness and fervor that I have never seen equalled or at least surpassed. The priests of the Snake Dance and the Lelentu (prayers for rain and that water will flow freely into the springs) are as earnest and sincere and devout as the most consecrated Christian minister or priest I ever saw. And the dancers of the Acomas, Lagunas, Hopis, Navahos, Zunis, etc., enter into these, their religious ceremonies, with an earnestness and reverence that put to shame the flippant, bustling, looking-around, whispering congregations of many of our so-called Christian churches.

THE ANTELOPE PRIEST PRAYING BEFORE THE SHRINE OF THE WEAVER OF THE CLOUDS.

Nor is this all. The Indian's every-day attitude is one of reverence for the Powers Above. He does everything with these before his mind. The first thing he does on awakening is to propitiate all the powers of the five or seven cardinal points. When the sun rises he makes his offering to the powers behind it, that control and direct it, that it may be a blessing throughout the day. Indeed, every act of his life may be said to have a religious thought attached to it, so powerfully is the religious instinct developed within him. If you offer him a cigarette he will propitiate the Powers Above and Around and Below before he

CARRYING THE SNAKES IN THEIR MOUTHS IN THE HOPI SNAKE DANCE.

gives himself up to the full enjoyment of it. He does this, however, with such apparent unconcern that the stranger would never dream of it, even though he were looking straight at him. But the knowing will understand. When he sees the Indian quietly blow a puff of smoke to the East, he knows that is for the purpose of reminding the good and evil powers that reside there that the smoker wishes their good influences to rest upon him, or, at least, that the evil influences shall pass him by. And the same thing when the smoker puffs to the North, the West, the South, and the *Here*. For the Navaho Indian believes that there are powers that need propitiating just here, while the Hopis add the powers of the Above and the Below, thus making seven cardinal points.

The secret prayers and rites of the underground kivas, or the medicine *hogans* of Hopi and Navaho are marvels of sincerity, earnestness, and reverence. One is impressed whether he understands them or not, and the white man comes away, or at least I do, with this feeling, viz., that I would to God the white race, so long as they worship at all, would do so with such outward decorum, reverence, and earnestness that would imply their real inward belief that the thing is more than a meaningless, perfunctory ceremony that they must go through.

Another remarkable thing I would that the white race would learn from the Indian is his habit of teaching the victim of a misfortune of birth that his misfortune is a mark of divine favor. Let me explain fully. A hunchback or a dwarf among the Indians is not made the butt of rude wit, ghastly jokes, or of cruel treatment, as is generally the case with such a one of our own race, but is treated with special consideration and kindness. I knew a Mohave boy who was humpbacked when born. The shaman or medicine man explained how the deformity came. He was a special child, a gift from the gods above. He came from the Above to the Here on the exquisite pathway of a rainbow. But, unfortunately, the rainbow rested over a very sharp, rugged mountain peak, which the gods did not see, and, as the child slid down to the earth, his poor, little, naked back caught on the sharp peak and was thus deformed. With such a story of his origin his parents were made happy, and as he grew older, he was treated with kindness and consideration by his boy companions. Now, while I would not gain

DRINKING THE EMETIC AFTER THE HOPI SNAKE DANCE.

this end by the superstitious story of the Mohave medicine man, I would that we could in some way teach our boys to look with compassion upon the misfortune of such as happen to be afflicted at birth, or to be light-witted, or in some way not the equal of the majority.

If an Indian be afflicted with hysteria, or fits of any kind, he is better treated as the result of his affliction rather than worse. Too often the white race makes these afflictions the cause of brutal and indifferent treatment, and adds sorrow to the already overburdened and distressed souls of the suffering.

CHAPTER XXVI

THE INDIAN AND IMMORTALITY

TO the materialist immortality is a foolish dream, to the agnostic an unjustified human craving, to the simple Christian a belief, and to the transcendentalist a confident hope, but to the Indian it is as positive an assurance as is life. The white race has complicated its belief in the future life with many theological dogmas. The Roman Catholic church has its purgatory, as well as its paradise and hell; the first as a place of purging for the sins committed in the body and that must be burned away, the second the abode of the blest, and the third the place into which the damned are cast. The Seventh Day Adventists believe that only those who are saved by "the blood of Christ" and obedience to his commands are blessed with the gift of immortal life. They contend it is a free gift as an act of God's grace and is not inherent in the soul or spirit of mankind. Those who refuse to accept salvation by the vicarious atonement of Christ, they believe, will be annihilated. The Presbyterian believes that a certain number of mankind are foreordained for salvation and heaven, and another number for damnation and hell, from the foundation of the world. The Universalist believes that all men will ultimately be saved and therefore enjoy heaven, whilst others have a belief in a "conditional" immortality.

The Indian believes in immortality without any admixture of complex theological ideas. His is a simple faith which he accepts as he accepts life. He believes that when he dies his spirit goes to its new life just as at birth he came into this life. And he believes that all the objects he used on earth — food, clothing, articles of adornment, baskets, horses, saddles, blankets — have a spirit-life as well as he has. Hence, when one dies, his friends throw upon his funeral pyre his clothing, blankets, and other personal belongings, utensils for his comfort, food for his nourishment on the way to the "under world," or land of the future, and strangle his horse that its spirit may aid him on his journey. When death approaches he faces it with calmness, equanimity and serenity. Fearless and unafraid he awaits the coming of the last great enemy. In effect, he cries out with Browning:

> "I would hate that death bandaged my eyes,
> And forbore, and bade me creep past.
> No! let me taste the whole of it; fare like my peers,
> The heroes of old."

No shirking for him; as calmly as Socrates took the bowl of fatal hemlock, the Indian awaits death and proudly passes on to the new life. Those who are left behind may wail for their loss, but the one who departs asks for and receives no sympathy.

Now, it is this simple acceptation of death as a natural thing that I would have the white race learn. And yet it can never come to us as an act of simple faith as it is with the Indian. Our civilization has spoiled us for "simple faith." That is practically impossible, save to a few souls who, unlike the rest of us, have "kept themselves unspotted from the world" of speculative thought, or theological dogma. It can come (and does with many) as the result of religious training, or as it did to Browning and Whitman. What wonderfully different minds these two men had. One an aristocrat, the other a democrat, yet both full of love for mankind, and each teaching with vigor and power the Fatherhood of God, the real brotherhood of man, and the immortality of the soul. Read Browning's *Prospice*, part of which I have already quoted, *Evelyn Hope*, *Abt Vogler*, and these three stanzas with which he opens his *La Saziaz*, and elsewhere calls a *Pisgah Sight*:

"Good, to forgive:
  Best, to forget!
  Living we fret;
Dying, we live.
Fretless and free,
  Soul, clap thy pinion!
  Earth have dominion,
Body, o'er thee!

Wander at will,
  Day after day,—
  Wander away,
Wandering still —
Soul that canst soar!
  Body may slumber:
  Body shall cumber
Soul-flight no more.

Waft of soul's wing!
  What lies above?
  Sunshine and Love,
Sky blue and Spring!
Body hides — where?
  Ferns of all feather,
  Mosses and heather,
Yours be the care!"

Compare these utterances with Whitman's rugged and forceful words:

"Passive and faltering,
The words, *the Dead*, I write,
For living are the Dead,
(Haply the only living, only real,
And I, the apparition, the spectre.)"

Again, in his *To One Shortly to Die*, what a triumphant note is in the last two lines:

"I exclude others from you, there is nothing to be commiserated,
I do not commiserate, I congratulate you."

How perfectly Indian, this attitude, this refusal to be sorry, and to offer congratulations rather than regrets. In his *Night on the Prairies* his perfect assurance as to the future is clearly expressed, and while measuring himself with the great thoughts of space and eternity that fill him as he gazes upon the myriads of globes above, he exclaims:

"Now I absorb immortality and peace, I admire death . . . .
O, I see now that life cannot exhibit all to me, as the day cannot,
I see that I am to wait for what will be exhibited by death."

In one poem he speaks of "awaiting death with perfect equanimity," and in another says:

"Thee, holiest minister of Heaven — thee, envoy, usherer, guide at last of all,
Rich, florid loosener of the stricture knot call'd life,
Sweet, peaceful, welcome Death."

And the reason for all this restfulness as to Death and the Future is expressed in his Assurances:

"I do not doubt that the passionately-wept deaths of young men are provided for, and that the deaths of young women and the deaths of little children are provided for. (Did you think life was so well provided for, and Death, the purport of all life, is not well provided for?)

I do not doubt that wrecks at sea, no matter what the horrors of them, no matter whose wife, child, husband, father, lover, has gone down, are provided for, to the minutest points.

I do not doubt that whatever can possibly happen anywhere, at any time, is provided for in the inherences of things.

I do not think Life provides for all, and for Time and Space, but I believe Heavenly Death provides for all."

So, reader, I care not how it comes into your soul, so that you have it there, a rich and precious possession, this living, active, potential belief in immortality. If you know *you are* now, and that you will never end, you will find that life itself becomes more enlarged and dignified. You will not be content with mere earthly aims, you will not rest satisfied to be a mere money-getter, but, realizing the immensity of your own capacities and powers, you will reach out for the eternal things, the realities that abide forever. For Joaquin Miller never wrote a truer word than when he said:

"For all you can hold in your dead cold hand,
Is what you have given away."

This forever settles a thoughtful man's conception of mere acquisitiveness. Such gatherings-together are unworthy the soul that feels and knows its own immortality. It needs a larger aim, a more worthy object.

Another thing in connection with what we call death, the white race may well learn from the Indian. How often does press and pulpit expend itself in finding superlatives to pour out in lavish eulogy over the dead, who, while alive, never did a thing to win the love of their fellows. Such eulogy in unknown among the Indians. The "preacher of an Indian funeral sermon" would no more dare wrongfully praise or laud his subject than he would falsely execrate him. He must speak the truth, the whole truth, and nothing but the truth, and while he is not called upon to expatiate upon the wrong-doings, the foibles or weaknesses of his subject, he must say no word of praise that is not justly earned and strictly true.

If this law were applied to the white race, what different funeral sermons and orations we should hear and read; and what different inscriptions we should read upon the tombstones found in our graveyards.

CHAPTER XXVII

VISITING THE INDIANS

OCCASIONALLY I meet with people who would like to visit real Indians in their real homes,— not the dressed-up Indians in a made home, like those of the Midway Plaisance of the World's Fair or of a "Wild West" show, and they ask me how they can do so. To the ordinary traveler of to-day, who requires all the comforts of a Pullman and a dining car, and who is not willing to forego them for the hardships of a camping-out trip, my advice is don't, although the hardships are more so in name than in fact. If one likes old clothes, fresh air, the great outdoors, lots of sunshine, desert roads, and meals *al fresco*,— sleeping at night under the stars,— this is just the country for such things. Given a good team, a careful driver who can cook "frontier style," and an agreeable traveling companion, and you will have a new thrill — no matter what the weather is. Five dollars a day each person will cover average cost of outfit; meals extra.

Yet there are some Indians who may be seen without leaving the luxuries of our modern civilization. Two great railway systems in our Southwest pass through the regions where live the Indians to whom I have referred in the foregoing pages. These are popularly known as the "Santa Fe" and the "Southern Pacific."

In crossing the continent from Chicago to the Pacific Coast on the Santa Fe route, one strikes the "Indian country," to which I refer, about half a day before reaching Albuquerque, New Mexico. Here is what might be termed "the heart of the Pueblo Indian country." The word "pueblo" is Spanish for "town," so the name merely means the stay-at-home town Indians as distinguished from the nomad or wandering tribes of the great plateaus.

At Albuquerque one may see, in Fred Harvey's collection in the Mission-style depot, a rare and precious gathering of Indian baskets, blankets, silverware, etc., that is one of the finest in the West. It ranks with the highest, and was largely gathered and placed under the personal direction of Dr. George A. Dorsey, the eminent ethnologist of the Field Columbian Museum. Nearly all the pueblos may be reached with this city as a radiating center, though Taos and the Indian villages of the northern Rio Grande valley are more accessible from Santa Fe. Isleta and Laguna are passed a few miles further west. A three hours' drive from Laguna, by way of the Enchanted Mesa, brings you to the sky city of Acoma. Zuni is a day's stage ride south of Gallup, New Mexico. At Winslow, or Canyon Diablo, Arizona, one may leave the railway for the 70 or 90 mile ride across the Painted Desert to the region of the Hopis, the snake-dancing Indians to whom I have often referred. At Williams, a little further west, on the branch line to the Grand Canyon, one may visit the Havasupais, and at Kingman, the Wallapais. At Needles, on the Colorado River, the boundary line between Arizona and California, one may see the Mohaves, and on the river, reached by boat from Needles, some forty miles below, are the Chemehuevis. In California, on the San Diego branch of the Santa Fe, one may reach various villages of

Mission Indians; Pala, Rincon, and several others from Oceanside; and San Ysabel, Mesa Grande, Los Coyotes, etc., from San Diego by team to Warner's Ranch. Saboba is reached on the San Jacinto branch, and Temecula on the Temecula branch.

The Santa Fe passenger department publishes a beautifully illustrated and well written book on the Indians of the Southwest, and it is well worth sending fifty cents to their general offices in Chicago for a copy.

The Southern Pacific also passes through a country where many Indians reside. The Apaches are reached from several of their Arizona stations, and the Pimas and Maricopas from Phœnix. At Aztec a stage takes one to Palomas, where an interesting band of Apaches are to be seen. The Indian reservation for the Yumas is just across the railway bridge at Zuma, and from Mecca, near the Salton Sea, one may reach the desert Indian villages of Martinez, Agua Dulce, Santa Rosa, etc. Palm Springs is the station for the Palm Springs Indians, five miles away, and at Porterville, north of Los Angeles, one starts for the drive to the Yokuts and other basket-making Indians.

This brief chapter makes no pretense to full treatment. It is merely a suggestion of help to those who wish to follow the Indian to his real home.

CHAPTER XXVIII

CONCLUSION

IN the foregoing chapters I have attempted to present in helpful form ideas that have slowly sifted into my own mind as my contact with the Indian has become less formal and restrained. In my case "familiarity" has not "bred contempt." I have learned many, and to me most important, lessons. In the hurry and whirl of our money-mad age and our machine-driven civilization, we have scarce time to sit down calmly and contemplate anything, hence my earnest plea for a return to the simple things, to the outdoors, to the quiet contentment of the Indian. Doubtless I have often said things both crudely and harshly, but I can truthfully affirm that I have never intended to be harsh, though I am less careful that my utterances be polished and refined than that they should find lodgment in earnest hearts.

To those who are honest and sincere in their desire to get the good out of what I have said, the flaws in my work will be generously passed by, and kindly disregarded. I have felt too intensely in the writing of some of these chapters to be able to judge what I have written by the cool, critical standard of the rhetorician. I have learned from the Indian that the real thing to be desired in oratory is to get one's thought into the other man's mind and heart so that it will influence his action. This has been my aim in writing these pages; so, in conclusion,

CONCLUSION

I thank thee, dusky brother of the plains, the mountains, the forests, and the canyons, for this lesson and ali the other lessons you have taught me. I am grateful for the lessons of the higher civilization. I prize and treasure them, but equally am I under obligation to thee, thou red-skin, for recalling to me some primitive principles which civilization ignores at its peril.